This Is Life

*Love,
Aurelia
Lee*

This Is Life

ARVILLA FEE

Foreword by Robert C. Evans

RESOURCE *Publications* · Eugene, Oregon

THIS IS LIFE

Copyright © 2023 Arvilla Fee. All rights reserved. Except for brief quotations in critical publications or reviews, no part of this book may be reproduced in any manner without prior written permission from the publisher. Write: Permissions, Wipf and Stock Publishers, 199 W. 8th Ave., Suite 3, Eugene, OR 97401.

Resource Publications
An Imprint of Wipf and Stock Publishers
199 W. 8th Ave., Suite 3
Eugene, OR 97401

www.wipfandstock.com

PAPERBACK ISBN: 979-8-3852-0476-2
HARDCOVER ISBN: 979-8-3852-0477-9
EBOOK ISBN: 979-8-3852-0478-6

VERSION NUMBER 11/21/23

I dedicate this book to God, my strength, hope, and salvation. To my mom, Shirley; my sister, Carla; and my daughter, Jennica who read every poem I write and amaze me daily with their kindness, strength and resilience. To my husband, Jamie, who supports and loves me and our children like a champ, even when he's exhausted. I truly don't know what I would do without him. To the rest of my children: Kara (my sprite with a mind of her own), Kyle (who is such a loyal, kind soul), Alec (who can build anything like a true engineer), D'Andre (our strong-willed toddler who loves cheese and cowboy boots), and Armoni (who is a fierce pursuer of dreams). I'm so proud of them. God knew I needed this crew. To Kyle's beautiful other half, Stephanie, my adorable granddaughter, Embree, and baby Ryland on the way. To Armoni's beautiful other half, Kaitlyn and baby Elijah on the way. I will be hearing the pitter patter of little feet for years to come! To my brother, Rob, who tells me he's proud of me and sends me a text every day. To my dad, Ray, whose work ethic has been an iron pillar in my life! To Frank, Carla's other half, a fiery Italian who can work harder than men half his age. To Nathan, Jennica's other half, wearer of silly socks and drinker of coffee, may he keep pressing toward his goals. To Hunter, Jennica's best bud who loves hiking, perfect sandwiches, and music—may he always live life out loud. To my nieces (and great niece) Clarissa, Sabrina, and Kinley who are some of the most fierce women I know and the best travel companions around—may we have *many* more adventures together! To my great nephews, Liam and Brayden, twin travel guides who can eat more sushi, talk more (and make me laugh more) than any other young men I know. To my great nieces Jenah and Molly, two amazing, intelligent young ladies who fill me with pride and joy. To my nephew, Josh, who makes me feel like a rock star and who gives me hope that we still have a generation who don't get their news from social media. To my forever-friend, Brian who makes it possible to stay sane by helping out with D'Andre! To my dear friends and sisters-in-Christ whom I love and cherish daily. I can't even begin to name all of them, but they know who they are. To my former students with whom I've kept in touch—they are loved more than they know. To Robert Evans, *the best professor I never had* (a little joke of ours). I'm grateful for our friendship and his incredible wisdom. And last, to my sweet dog, Rio, who got hit and killed by a car on April 5, 2023. That horrible day is forever etched in my mind and has left an aching void in my heart. Perhaps someday my new puppy, Max will begin to fill that space (after he stops chewing on the carpet and biting my hand).

CONTENTS

Foreword by Robert C. Evans	xiii
Preface	xvii
This is Life	xix

Part I | Jagged Edges

And the World Moves On	3
April Ashes	4
The Art of Mourning	6
Battles Unseen	7
Blue Black Hours	8
Brain Storm	9
Don't Die on Me	10
Getting Orders	12
The Great Divide	14
The Great Pretending	15
Grief	16
Happiness is a Choice	17
I Am Nobody	18
I Carry the Weight	19
In This God-Forsaken Place	20
Journey through Meth	21
A Little Lazarus	22
Masquerade	23
The Mourning Road	24
No New Normal	25
Not the Only One	26
The Other Side	27
Put a Pin in It	28
Ruins	29
That Moment	30

Contents

There Used to be a Garden	31
Those Remember Days	32
Time	33
When Doves Cry	34

Part II | It's Complicated

All that Remains	37
All that You Were	38
Beware the Counterfeits	39
Body Language	41
Candles	42
The Cycle	43
The Drought	44
The Fatted Calf	45
Flash in the Pan	46
Flight Risk	47
Full of Yourself	49
Gaunt	50
Left to Dry	51
Location	52
Nothing at All	53
Primitive	54
Remember	55
Sister Long Gone	56
Square Pegs	58
Truth be Told	59
Untethered	61
Water Fresh and Salt	62
We Opened a Joint Account	63
What Lies Beneath	64
You Wore Religion	65

Part III | Low Battery

Aren't We All a Little Bit Mad?	69
Between	70

CONTENTS

Did I Sleep	71
Driving Blindfolded	72
Empty	73
Fresh Out	74
Galaxies	75
Hitchhiking to the Stars	76
Imagining a Slow Down	77
Left Hanging	78
Lord I'm Tired	79
The Razor's Edge	80
Redial	81
Today	82
What the World Sees	83

Part IV | As the Days Go By

Aging: Not for the Faint of Heart	87
Carry the Wish Seed	88
Church Campground Reunion	89
The Decline of Old Detroit	91
The Edge of Remembering	92
Forgive Me If	94
Grandma's Sunday Kitchen	95
How to Anti-Age Gracefully	96
Life Defined	97
The Lovely Janitor	98
Nostalgia for Nostalgia's Sake	100
What Did You Do with the Dash?	102
When I Grow Old	104
You Can't Take it with You	105

Part V | The Bigger World

Actions Speak Louder	109
Chasing the Unicorn	110
Civilization	111
Corner of Fifth and Main	113

ix

Contents

Count the Seconds, Divide by Five	114
Cracks in Humanity	115
Decay	116
A Different Kind of Hunger	117
Expendables	118
From a Former Skeleton	119
Genetics	120
Left Field	121
Lessons from Mrs. P	122
Listening	123
Melting Down	124
Mouths in Motion	125
No Common Ground	126
Origami	127
Rabbit	129
Silencer	130
The Sound of Silence	132
Stained Glass Prayers	133
State of the Human Address	135
We Came Back	137
When I Grow Up	138
The World is Cancelled Today	140

Part VI | Natural Remedies

Beach Mornings	143
Breakthrough	145
Lake Erie in Ashtabula	146
Lake Triolet	147
Life in the Cracks	148
Ocean Triolet	149
Pilgrimage	150
Porch Summers	151
River for Keeps	152
The Self-Made Poet	153
Stopping in the Woods with Frost	155
Summer Triolet	156

Contents

Under the Canopy	157
When Foxes Play	159
Writing Muses	160

Part VII | Laughter is the Best Medicine

Before Social Media	163
Family Reunion	164
Hats off to	165
I Heard a Fly Buzz	166
I Named Him Patrick	168
Measuring Stick	170
A Memorial Service for Memory	171
Out of Order	172
The Pros and Cons of Love Explained in Twenty Lines	174
Read the Sign	175

Part VIII | The Way Back

The Art of Being	179
Been a Long Time Coming	180
Fanning the Flames	182
The Grand Escape	183
Make Space	184
Not in My DNA	185
Patched	186
Remote Control	187
Sweeping	188
A Time to Burn	189
Today I Will Eat Potato Chips	190
Where I Belong	191
Who Says	193
Without Saying a Word	194
Acknowledgements	195
About the Author	201

FOREWORD

This is the second book of poems I have read by Arvilla Fee, and it is the second that has greatly impressed me by its themes, its messages, its diversity of ideas and experiences, and, above all, by its sheer *poetic* quality. Without that last-mentioned trait, all the others are relatively insignificant. When I was a student long ago, there was a wonderful little book, often used in classes dealing with poetry, titled *How Does a Poem Mean?* Not "what does a poem mean," but *how*. Poetry, perhaps more than any of the other literary arts, is the most dense, the most compact, the one in which each single word and sound carries the most resonance and is therefore under the most pressure. And, precisely for these reasons, it is, I would argue, the most *difficult* of the literary arts to master. Well, Arvilla Fee has mastered it. In poem after poem, both in her first book and in this one, she has made every single word and every individual sound count, and she has also (another important skill) shown herself a master of literary forms. I say "forms" (with an *s*) because poems exist not only as words and sounds but also as shapes, even when they sometimes seem relatively straightforward and shapeless. In this book, you will encounter brief lyrics with short lines, lengthy "prose poems" with tight, short twists at their conclusions, and a variety of other forms that show Arvilla Fee to be inventive not only in the individual phrases she uses but in the variety of forms she imposes on (or, better, discovers for) her material.

Let me illustrate a few examples of the varied successes of these poems. In the very first lyric, for instance, we hear a poet playing with alliteration and near-rhyme ("The smu*dges* / the rough e*dg-es*"), with assonance, alliteration, and near-rhyme combined ("the *rain* / on window*panes*"), with striking imagery ("lightning forked / into *tridents*"), and with paradox ("of deception and truth"). And all these varied "sound effects" appear just in the poem's first ten lines. And then, as is so utterly typical of this collection, the opening poem concludes with the kind of reversal that implies this poet's

xiii

FOREWORD

craft in creating a stunning "sense of an ending," to quote from the title of another important book. Listen to how the first poem comes, not to a rest, but to a twist:

> Sidewalks scorched
> beneath suns,
> hearts undone;
> yet a flower
>   grows
> through the cracks.

Nothing in the sounds of the preceding five lines prepares us for the surprise of "cracks," just as the strength of the flower described is similarly unexpected. And, to note just one further detail about this promising opening poem, note how the poet sets the key verb—"grows"—emphatically off by itself in a single line. This is a writer who either knows what she is doing, word-by-word, or who is inspired by some unselfconscious power, or, more probably, both at once.

This poet's lyrics are full of sharply observant images, as in the claim that Time "does not let you rest / in its pockets"—two lines which, by the way, illustrate this poet's skill at subtle enjambment (running one line into the next without punctuation). Or consider another vivid bit of imagery: "the earth still turns" (note the assonance and alliteration) "spilling people sideways" (an alliterative phrase with a memorable image) "around its blue-green globe" (more alliteration, and what a striking image, too!). This, sad to say, is the kind of poetic skill that probably cannot be taught (otherwise there would be many more talented poets than there are). It has to be, to some extent, and innate gift, and these poems by this poet display that gift in almost every single instance.

There is a wonderful music in many of these poems, and the music, which appeals to our inner ears, is often combined with images that appeal to our inner eyes, as in such phrases as "all colliding under a steel-gray sky," or "their soft coo-coos unobtrusive," or "limbs held in a watery vice," or "concaving the heart, / hollowing the stomach," or . . . or . . . or . . . One could easily go on, listing example after example, but to do that would be to deny readers the

xiv

FOREWORD

pleasure of the many impressive surprises that await them as they peruse this wonderful book.

Robert C. Evans
Emeritus Professor of English /
Auburn University at Montgomery

PREFACE

"Words can be like X-rays if you use them
properly—they'll go through anything.
You read and you're pierced."

—ALDOUS HUXLEY, BRAVE NEW WORLD

I may not be a math guru or understand the intricacies of chemistry, but one of the most natural things in the world for me is to express life through a deliberate arrangement of words. From the time I learned to read and write, which I suppose was around first grade, I've been using words to capture the things I see and feel. I learned early on that one of the most powerful forms of written expression is poetry—an itty bitty package with a mighty big punch.

Like the poems from my first book, *The Human Side*, many of the poems contained in *This is Life* stem from my own experiences. Some of these pieces were written with tears running down my face, others were written in a state of exhaustion, depression, or reflection. Life is messy, complicated, and full of plot twists. We're not always honest with those around us because it's easier to say, "I'm fine," and press on. How do we tell people we are at the end of our ropes? That we grieve so much we can barely breathe? That we are getting older and ache in places we didn't know we had? How do we end toxic relationships? What do we do when we are overwhelmed by political wranglings and the tragic events happening in our society? Where do we go when we need peace? It is my hope that the poems in this book can help provide context to some of these questions and give readers the sense they are not alone in their struggles. One of the best compliments I've ever received about my writing was from someone who said, "You gave me the words I couldn't say."

And while you might need a few tissues—these poems cover more than burdens and heartache. Many of them are about finding

Preface

solace in nature, finding relief through laughter, and about the indelible human spirit to overcome whatever is thrown our way.

Blessings to all,
Arvilla

THIS IS LIFE

The smudges,
the rough edges,
parts that scrape,
make you bleed,
leave scars.
The rain
on windowpanes,
lightning forked
into tridents
of deception and truth.
Hairpin turns
around S curves,
falling rocks,
the debris of grief
in caves.
Sidewalks scorched
beneath suns,
hearts undone;
yet a flower
         grows
through the cracks.

PART I

Jagged Edges

AND THE WORLD MOVES ON

Time does not pause;
it does not let you rest
in its pockets;
the sun still rises and sets,
oblivious to the tear stains
on your pillowcase;
the earth still turns,
spilling people sideways
around its blue-green globe;
the wind still blows scraps
of your life across the yard;
laughter still floats
through the air,
though you can't absorb
the grating sound of it.
Tis the way of grief, love,
that space of being
yet not being,
days blurring together,
reality slipping
through your hands
in an attempt
to grasp an illusion.

APRIL ASHES

"April is the cruellest month"
T.S. Eliot, *The Wasteland*

Eliot wasn't wrong,
not in his time,
not in mine.
April brought rain,
a speeding car,
my dog running—
all colliding under a steel-gray sky.
My feral screams
broke April into pieces.
April dripped
from the ends of my hair,
soaked my jeans,
soaked the fur of my sweet boy.
He wouldn't have liked that.
The driver picked up a piece
of his bumper, said sorry.
April isn't sorry enough.
I couldn't accept;
I had to wrap a still body
in a towel, had to hold him
and say no—no, no, no, no.
Had to grasp a paw gone cold.
Had to load his body in my car,
travel to the crematorium.
Had to listen to reassurances,

as if April could ever be a balm.
There is a box
sitting on the mantle now.
It does not sit on my lap.
April is silence.
April is ashes.

THE ART OF MOURNING

Perhaps doves have mastered grief
best, their soft coo-coos unobtrusive
yet so categorically solemn,
a sound that pierces even the foggiest
mornings, a mourning of what, I don't know.
But I want to take lessons, write it all down,
want to know how to walk on two legs,
pecking at seeds on the ground—even
in the rain. I want to be able to lift my wings,
to rise and let the wind guide me to a nest
where, no matter the weather, I will continue
to build, continue to produce new life.

BATTLES UNSEEN

We creep along the walls
camouflaged faces—
painted to chameleon
our surroundings;
perhaps our bright smiles
will be among thousands;
no one will see the darkness
hidden behind our eyes.
It's easy enough to deflect
How are you
when two words cover
an entire battleground;
I'm fine.
And so our secrets remain
tucked behind the bulwarks
where the only true enemy
holds hostage our minds.

BLUE BLACK HOURS

Sometimes, in the blue-black hours just before dawn,
when my head is still wrapped in the gossamer gauze

of half sleep, I forget where I am—who I am, and peace
shrouds my consciousness for that one blessed moment—

gone is the barbed pain that burrows into my heart
when I think about how you slipped away from earth,

so tenuous was the thread and its gravitational hold;
no amount of pleading could revoke your release,

your floating beyond those undiscovered galaxies;
I know my screams did not reach your ears gone cold,

but I screamed anyway because what else does one do?
In a state of awakeness, I can never shed the skin of grief;

so, I revel in the blue-black hours, that hazy mist between
what's real and make-believe. I choose to stay just beneath

the surface, where I often see your eyes staring back at me,
and I can draw in a breath through lungs not made of stone.

BRAIN STORM

Darkness is split only by jagged
tridents of lightning,
thunder rumbles in my chest;
I hold my breath,
anticipating the next wave.
It crashes over my head;
I'm washed under,
limbs held in a watery vise.
My lungs burn from unreleased
air; my feet find no purchase;
then I bob to the surface again
choking, gasping, my body spent.
I'll just let go, I think,
sink into oblivion, a land of peace.
When I awake, my mouth tastes
of sand and hope, and I blink against
pale rays of sun. I'm taped to an IV drip;
they tell me I'm going to be just fine.

DON'T DIE ON ME

Don't die on me in the spring
when the earth turns green
and robins sing of hope.
When buds unfurl and grace
the world with perfume,
and the sun's thin rays
grow more brave and thaw
each hardened heart.

Don't die on me in the summer
amid fields of clover
when the birds and bees join
flowers and trees
giving life to the earth, a rebirth
beneath a cotton-candy sky
where the sun hangs high
warming our souls.

Don't die on me in the fall
when the trees stand tall
dressed for the ball in reds
and dazzling golds, when
cold rains come and leaves
are done, sitting in sad piles
on the ground, the feel
of frost in the air.

Don't die on me in the winter,
when my heart will splinter
like a pond, just-iced in snow.
I'll have nowhere to go;
in a world so low, hands frozen,
breath steaming the air. Don't
you dare leave me alone
to face the cold.

Don't die on me.

GETTING ORDERS

The sound packing tape makes
as it spins off the spool
onto a cardboard box—
got to admit I have a little PTSD
from that sound, so it's a good thing
I can't write it down.
Down to the last box,
staring at the empty nail holes
in the drywall, remembering pictures
we hung there—what, just three years ago?
I'll miss the way the golden light filtered in
through the tall French doors;
we'd never had French doors before.
Seems odd to close a door you'll never open
again, but we do it all the time. Well, not all
the time, but every three-four years or so.
So, here we go again. Truck is loaded. Our lives
are in the back of a truck, bumping along
the country to their next destination.
Not a destination we chose, per se, although
they had us fill out a wish list of places
we'd like to live. That's all it is—just wishes
because the government's going to do
what it likes. Perhaps we should try reverse
psychology sometimes—say we want Minot
so they'll send us to Hickam. We put the car
in reverse; I see the kids looking out the back
window. It's hard on them, hard on us. All this

saying goodbye and weeping, and leaving
flowers we planted in a yard that was never ours.
We never stay planted.

THE GREAT DIVIDE

An earthquake,
a continental shift,
a break in time
so complete,
so final
that no bridge
can span the gap
between before and after.
Each memory
now has a category
that falls completely
on one side or the other.
Then.
Now.
The heart can heal
but cannot erase the line.
A demarcation
drawn in permanent marker.

THE GREAT PRETENDING

I'm fine, I tell people,
and by all accounts,
I look fine.
Fine is automatic—
a practiced smile,
a voice stripped
of emotion.
They don't need to see
        inside,
no sense in letting them
wander through the maze
like mice looking for cheese,
bumping into the what ifs.
They would have words—
meant to sooth and heal,
and I would nod
like I understand
then I would wait
until I was alone
and sob like a child
whose balloon is now
        lost—
a splotch of red
against the steel-gray sky.

GRIEF

raw
cutting edges,
a thousand blades,
concaving the heart,
hollowing the stomach;
it's a ball
without beginning
without end,
a circular pain
that stems
from a single moment
in time,
one that cannot be undone
no matter how much pain
is spent on the wishing.

HAPPINESS IS A CHOICE

Happiness is a choice, they say. Sure it is. Until it's not. Until the door is opened, and your dog, your best furry friend in the entire world, goes bolting out, straight into an on-coming car. Until you are kneeling in the rain over his dead body screaming a scream so primal, so feral that you don't even know it's coming out of you. Until tears and rain streak your face as you wrap his body in a towel then stand there holding him for ages, numbly, dumbly because you have no idea what else to do. *Happiness is a choice.* Until it's not. Until you load him in the back of your minivan and drive him to the crematorium. Until you hold his paw one last time, knowing the next time you see him, he will be in a sealed box. Ashes. Funny, how you just can't choose to look away from his pictures. How you just can't unsee the scene that ended his life. How the replays and regrets are on a constant film loop inside your mind. *Happiness is a choice.* Until it's not. Until you weep wracking sobs because he's no longer looking up at you with his adoring golden-brown eyes. Because he's no longer lying beside you when you take a nap. Because his toys are in a bag, his empty leash hanging from a hook in the laundry room. You don't choose the pain, the weight that sits on your chest like a rogue elephant. You don't choose loss. *Happiness is a choice*; until it's not.

I AM NOBODY

My eyes move across her page,
shy student, sits in the back,
never speaks.

But yet, here is her assignment,
speaking.
Who Am I Essay:

I am silence
I am invisible
I am alone
I am wallpaper
I am a guitar without strings
I am a fish out of the pond
I am an unwritten song
I am broccoli, no cheese
I am a dandelion in a rose garden
I am a mirage in the desert
I am nothing
I am Nobody

I hold her honesty
in my hands
like shattered egg shells.

I CARRY THE WEIGHT

of my students,
the weight of their grades,
yes, of course,
but also the weight
of their success
in life as well as school,
the weight of their hunger,
as many do not have food,
the weight of their sadness,
as many have no parents
encircling them with arms
of love,
the weight of their fears
as many walk the streets
fraught with danger—bullets
that do not miss their mark,
the weight of their dreams,
as many cannot look into a mirror
and see a star-filled sky
reflected back at them.

IN THIS GOD-FORSAKEN PLACE

When I held your little hand
and pointed out wild daisies

while we walked, you never said
I'll be an addict when I grow up.

Would I have changed anything
had I known you'd tumble down

the rabbit hole and sip cups of tea
with the maddest of Mad Hatters?

Could I have shouted louder?
Prayed harder? Turned you away

from the grinning Cheshire cat?
I barely recognized your body

the day they loaded up the gurney
and recited time of death;

your lips were as blue
as an Alice dress.

JOURNEY THROUGH METH

the skin on her face,
once a beautiful plain
full of blush and promise,
contoured cheekbones,
lips parted to show
an even row of white teeth,
but that was before—
before a chemical
burned its way through
her blood cells, her bones,
before unseen bugs
crawled beneath her skin,
made her itch, scratch—
scratch that beautiful face
now sallow, sunken,
sores on skeletal cheekbones,
lips picked raw,
and, when parted into a smile,
black holes in place of teeth.

A LITTLE LAZARUS

My face feels wet, but I can't work out why—or where I am. My eyelids are weighted, as though compressed with sand bags. It must be morning; light shines outside my closed lids. I hear voices. *Ma'am, can you hear me? Ma'am, are you okay?* I want to answer, but my tongue lies thick and flat in my mouth—has it grown roots? The notion makes me laugh, although the sound is that of an ancient bullfrog. Voices again—*she's coming around.* Hours later I lie under warm white sheets, the smell of antiseptic and sterile latex gloves beneath my nose. They tell me I'm in the hospital. I overdosed. I'm also under arrest—enough heroin in my pocket to charge me with "intent to distribute." And, yes, I'd had intent. I remember now. My buyers were coming; I took a hit while waiting. Waiting, as it turns out, is the hardest part as I now sit in my 6 x 8 cell. I'm clean—by force. But you know, it feels good. I've stopped shaking; I no longer claw at bugs. Preacher man paid me a visit last week and gave me a Bible. Seems like there might be something to this Jesus thing.

stone removed
my fingertips trace
this second skin

MASQUERADE

We pass each other in the store,
a quick hello near organic carrots;
we see each other in Sunday pews,
our eyes shuttering the truth.
It's easier this way—to carry on
as though we're dressed to the nines
at a masquerade ball, never revealing
our faces behind the masks. Clever,
aren't we? The way we hide our bruises,
the cuts on our battered hearts and wrists?
We nod and say we're fine because well,
it's easier, truth be told. Truth be told,
it's easier to lie. For if the masks slip,
what horrors would be revealed?
Are there enough psychotherapists
to go around?

THE MOURNING ROAD

1

watch out for those S curves
something coming around the bend;
hug the wall of the cliff
unless you're afraid of falling rocks;
I guess it's either rocks or a head-on
collision; take your pick

2

that long stretch of highway
across the flatlands, not a tree
in sight; staring blankly, eyes heavy,
the yellow line a broken ribbon
giving permission to pass other cars,
but there are no others

3

rain-soaked asphalt, lights a blur,
trying to stay between the lines,
white-knuckled grip on the steering
wheel; wipers, even a full speed,
cannot keep up with the deluge of tears
pouring from a purple sky

NO NEW NORMAL

A glass shatters on the floor,
not the kind of break
one might glue back together,
but tiny shards that scatter
in all directions,
shards I might find months later,
under the fridge, the stove.
You'll find a new normal, they say.
But I don't know how;
so many pieces are missing,
pieces of you that lie in ashes,
in a box on my mantle,
pieces imprinted on my arm
in your paw-shaped tattoo.
There is no new normal;
there's only a space beside me
where you used to be.

NOT THE ONLY ONE

"No man is an island entire of itself; every man
is a piece of the continent, a part of the main"
~John Donne, 1624

Curled inside pain,
alone in the dark
save for pinpricks of stars
is anyone there—
where?
Tears carve a valley
in her stricken face,
shame the shackles
that bind her feet
into place; she has died
and survived, has been a lie
to the lies; the tally marks
of failure on cave walls,
a statistic, a study in the arts
of possession; she has a confession:
this is not who I am;
I have a heart; I'm the sum of my
parts; my blood bleeds as red;
I'm part of the thread, the fabric
of your life. I'm not the only one,
at the end of my rope; tell me
there's hope. Tell me I'm a piece
of the continent, a part of the main.

THE OTHER SIDE

Three seconds. That's all I need back. I would keep him from running into the street. I held him, rain soaking my hair, unwilling to let go. I'm hollow, scraped out like a bowl. Bowl. His bowls are gone. His toys are in the attic. Toys. I found his favorite toy under my bed, his yellow Peep. Yellow, the color of flowers in April. I took him to the crematorium today. The man promised to be kind. Kind. I held onto his paw one last time and wept until I bent in two. I can't seem to uncurl from my grief. Grief. A thousand jagged edges.

before and after,
chasm
without a bridge

PUT A PIN IN IT

This grief,
open and raw—
the kind that makes
my throat ache,
my chest as thick
as dark molasses.
Oh, that I could
put a pin in it –
save it for a rainy day,
come back and touch
this purple bruise
to see if it still hurts.

RUINS

Once the home of Lords and Kings,
now a sprawling mess of stones,

yet somehow beautiful, for much
can be seen by squinting the eyes

and tilting the head; look—
there was a courtyard, a church;

the bells once rang from towers
where birds now build their nests,

and I can't help but wonder
if people would pay to see the ruins

of me; look—there are flowers
growing through the cracks of time;

there's a cast-iron song just above
the pigeon dung.

THAT MOMENT

right before the other shoe drops,
right before that pivot,
a glass yet unbroken,
a dog not yet hit by a car,
a teen pregnancy left unspoken—
right before the world tilts sideways,
right before that midnight phone call,
a heart still beating,
a body not yet found,
a laugh not yet extinguished—
right before color drains from your face,
right before dropping into the abyss,
a truck not yet rounding the curve,
a boy hesitating in front of a dealer,
an ambulance not in route.

THERE USED TO BE A GARDEN

Flowers once stood,
leaves outstretched
to embrace the sun;
the soil held earthy
promises
buried in catacombs
of worms.
Days were warm;
the breeze blew kisses
       —until
the sadness came,
drawing a curtain
across the sun;
the flowers wept
velveteen petals,
their salt tears
giving birth to weeds.

THOSE REMEMBER DAYS

There are days that stretch
like warm taffy,
but they are not sweet,
only sticky.
Sticky with memories
that slice time
into before and after—
memories so sharp
they've carved
into your mind
what hour the call came,
what you were wearing,
the way the room tilted
sideways—heavy with news.
They say grief is five stages,
and yet we never conquer
the stage that makes us
look at the calendar,
draw in a deep breath,
and hold our hands
over our hearts.

TIME

is not linear;
it twists around
to scratch an unreachable
itch,
collapses in on itself
at the mere mention
of a name,
the notes of a song,
the smell of hyacinths
in spring.
Time does not always
march forward
but retreats
into the darkest corners,
sitting among cobwebs of grief,
rocking back and forth
on its heels,
clutching unexplainables.
Time is a chasm of sleep,
until it steps, unexpectedly,
into yellow sunlight
and blinks
at a day not yet spent.

WHEN DOVES CRY

that mournful sound
echoing through the chimney flu
on a mist-covered morning
before the sun has yet to burn away
the remnants of a heavy night—
and you, eyes still closed,
still burrowed in a feathered nest,
before memories scramble for purchase
in your sleep-sludged brain,
that one twig-thin slice of time
where you forget about the loss
that has fissured your heart like dirt cakes
baked too long in the sun, awaiting rain
that never comes.

PART II

It's Complicated

ALL THAT REMAINS

Will you carry my memories
with the change in your pocket?
Will I drift on the tendrils of smoke
exhaled from your cigarettes?
Will I stare up at you
from the depths of your coffee
cup? Do you still drink it black?
Will you visit our old haunts?
See my reflection in the window
of that darling bakery on 45th?
Will you weep when you butter
your toast because you are truly
the worst butterer in the world?
Will you star gaze in your boxers
from your fourth-floor balcony?
Will my voice rise from the street
and rest like a feather in your hair?

ALL THAT YOU WERE

Fingers as small
as fairy wings,
delicate rose-petal
eyelids that remain
closed,
light blue veins
under paper-thin skin,
light blue lips,
which I kiss
a dozen times
before they tell me
it's time for me
to let go;
but how can I?
My breasts ache,
and I taste salt
from my tears.
As long as I hold you,
I can pretend
you are warm,
pretend I am still
the mother
who can keep you
safe and take you
home.

BEWARE THE COUNTERFEITS

Her momma warned her
when she moved to the city,
Not every purse sold on the streets
is real Gucci,
but they sure look good.
What she should have told her
is that not every man
with a table full of purses
is a real salesman,
but they sure look good too.
That's the first lesson a country girl
learns while staring out a porthole
with a faux city view from a studio
that has brick walls inside and out,
while beans cook on a stove
with one working burner
and the radiator hisses like a cat
until you give it a good kick.
But she'll learn;
she'll turn bruises into brass;
she'll nickel and dime it
and claw her way through
art school until she's produced
genuine gallery pieces,
until she has a real Gucci purse
slung over her shoulder

and a string of broken hearts
trailing from the bottom
of her red high heels.

BODY LANGUAGE

How strange to see such frigidity
in the sultry heat of a baked July,
but there they were, sitting apart
on a once-green park bench
as though they might get cooties
should their shoulders meet.
They were together;
two strangers would have little
reason to stretch their mouths
into thin, disapproving lines
and cast occasional fish hook
glances like they were hoping
for a bite.

CANDLES

How briefly they burn
wax trickling down
the sides,
      tears of loss,
beaten down, bankrupt,
flame flickering, wavering
         with each gust,
bending, regaining rigidity,
bending again,
      wicks blackened by time,
by carbon
your carbon and mine,
smudged shadows on the wall, an attempt
to make us bigger than we are,
      hot wells recessed,
how little wick is left
         to kiss the match
that keeps us burning.

THE CYCLE

Words hurled against the wall,
breaking like glass plates,
shards around her shoulders.
She cringes, retreats to a fox hole
for the duration of the battle.
She'll bear the bruises tomorrow,
but no one will know behind layers
of foundation and her crooked smile.
She's good like that—changing her coat
to white when faced with winter snow.
Only her eyes tell a different story,
but who looks at eyes anymore
since most reside on mobile islands,
too busy to spare a glance?
So, she'll carry on, stiff upper lip
and all; she'll return home to flowers
and apologies—each lavishly lined
with manipulation. Then she'll don
an apron and stand ramrod straight
as he hugs her from behind—knowing
she's one misplaced salad fork
from rinse and repeat.

THE DROUGHT

The grass died that summer,
unnatural wheat-colored patches
that crunched underfoot
beneath a mid-July sun;
everyone prayed for rain,
but clouds were sparse,
afraid to challenge shimmers
of heat that rose like specters
from gummy asphalt.
I tried to keep hydrated,
but my own yard fissured;
my bones turned to dust
during stilted conversations,
meals eaten in sulky silence.
How long has it been
since we've had a proper downpour,
a real, come-to-Jesus meeting
with lightning and thunder?
I try to remember as I dab my face
with a cool cloth.
Is that your car I see coming
down the driveway
or a mirage?

THE FATTED CALF

I watched you walk away
with a defiant flip
of your honey-blond ponytail;
part of me envied you,
the way you stood up
to the big man,
taking your inheritance
without a second glance.
You were gone for years,
but I kept his laundry clean,
washed every single dish.
So, I didn't understand
his frantic race down the lane
when he saw you coming home,
the way he fussed over you,
drawing a bath, laying out a robe.
He told me to fix steaks that night
—steaks, dear sister,
with roasted potatoes in olive oil,
and salad greens with feta cheese—
I guess the child who sleeps with pigs
receives the better feast.

FLASH IN THE PAN

The phone rings. We knew the call was coming, but knowledge does not soften the blow of the case worker's words: *we'll need you to bring him to the agency tomorrow, 11 a.m.* My mind replays the last 28 days in quick succession: that first night he arrived with nothing but the clothes on his back and a bottle. Holding, singing, midnight feedings. . .bright blue eyes staring up at us with questions. He must've wondered where his parents were, and oh, how I wanted to erase his trauma, to never let him feel the pain of bad decisions that were not his own. 28 days. We give him one last bath, dress him one last time. Kiss little cheeks we'll never kiss again. His grandma is waiting, like a bull in a corral, nostrils flaring—angry at a system that includes our family. As she snatches him away, we stand there numbly, hot tears streaking our faces. Without a backward glance, she's gone, and there's nothing left to do but return home. Silence sits in each room. Toys he'd played with. Clothes he'd worn. We pick them up, one-by-one without speaking.

time slips
through the minute holes,
distant chimes

FLIGHT RISK

I see myself now in the same state of disrepair
as the cottage you kept by the sea,

the one with the little white gate hanging askew
on one exhausted bolt,

the one with paint peeling from the door, limp
strands of cornflower blue.

I became aware, too late, you had the attention
span of a gnat,

that the crumbling petals I found near the base
of an ornate vase

presented a perfectly framed cameo of all that
you are and will ever be:

an unmade bed, discarded clothes, mold setting
up camp on long-forgotten cheese,

an unwatered garden, roses clinging desperately
to a trellis shanked by wind.

You like the idea of things—those chic intangibles
like love, goodwill and harmony,

but give you a toothache, a lawn to mow, a baby
to cry on your shoulder,

and you scamper towards life's nearest off-ramp,
legs spinning, dust flying,

making the best excuses, which the wind carries
back to my abandoned ears.

FULL OF YOURSELF

The temperature rises
the moment you step
through the doorway.
Like a hot-air balloon,
you float above the crowd,
your cocksure voice
drowns out the music;
the people who laugh
at your jokes are unaware
of your keen manipulation,
and as long as they think
you are the smartest person
in the room, you will never
get blown off course.

GAUNT

Look how thin we've become,
the ribs of our relationship,
the clavicle of our complacency,
on display for the world to see.
When did we stop eating?
Was it the year we decided
to abandon our éclairs in France
and eat salads in Pittsburg instead?
Was it those protein breakfast shakes,
each of us trying to out-health the other?
Was it that year our plates never touched
the table at the same time, hurried, half-
eaten sandwiches as we burnt our calories
faster than we burnt money and the time
spent making it? Your sea-foam-colored eyes
barely glance at me, studiously avoiding
the gauntness of my cheeks, the way I pick
sesame seeds from a bun. Why not sit down,
love? Shall we share a slice of chocolate cake
for old time's sake?

LEFT TO DRY

You didn't need to hang me
out to dry;
the desert sun would have
crept through the windowpanes,
skittered along the floor,
and found me where I lay prone
across the bed.
But perhaps you liked the view
of me twisting in the wind,
gained some sort of satisfaction
knowing I was pinned to the line,
and that only you
could take me down
and carry me into the house,
stiff as Egyptian papyrus.

LOCATION

Where are my shoes?
In the shoe bin.
I can't find my pencils!
They're on the table.
I've lost my favorite t-shirt!
Dresser, third drawer down.

If only it was still that easy,
that mother's knack
of knowing where everything
is—a dolphin's echolocation
for each missing item.

But the questions grew harder:
Where is my place in the world?
Where is the God of my youth?

I frantically search for answers
as my daughter combs the globe
for her soul.

NOTHING AT ALL

Blank.
Numb.
Weightless.
Her eyes look at me
but see nothing;
she's swimming
in the heroin sea,
playing the mermaid,
wrapping herself
in seaweed.
Pupils dilated,
she's down,
sedated,
chillest of chill.
She says *I love you*,
and I know on another
day, that might be true.
But not today.
Today she loves nothing
but the euphoric high
squirted from the end
of a needle.

PRIMITIVE

Why do you choke on the words
I'm sorry
as though you just swallowed
the pit of a peach,
And how can you demand grace,
your arms crossed,
your feet planted like tree roots
while the notion of giving grace
is as foreign to you
as a peacock in pajamas?
You neither lie nor tell the truth,
just offer up cocktails
of mixed stories
with those tiny umbrellas on top.
And I'm supposed to sip and smile
and pretend like I'm having
the time of my life—
just so you can beat your neanderthal chest
and show off the prize you brought home.

REMEMBER

Remember when we talked,
darling? About everything always,
went on those boardwalk walks?

We'd laugh at the silliest things,
our shoulders bumping each other;
I'd double over when you tried to sing.

We'd race each other into the water,
legs halted by its density and depth,
mermaids bathing; the sun grew hotter.

Remember when we didn't talk,
darling? About anything, ever—
didn't take those boardwalk walks?

Our faces froze in mutual blame;
our shoulders rarely ever touched;
the jilted waves called our names.

Remember when I sailed away,
and you didn't try to make me stay?

SISTER LONG GONE

That chasm in your heart
with the missing pieces—
the piece that got the call,
the piece ensconced in grief,
the piece that couldn't believe
she was gone.
Daughter, mother, sister,
aunt, niece, friend—a
wardrobe of kindred souls
she filled with her light.
Gone.
And for what? A drug
that never erased pain,
never built the bridge,
to the road out of town—
that kept her dreams
just out of reach,
her fingertips empty.
Gone.
The what ifs haunt us
nine years later. Useless,
I know. A futile mind game
that will never bring her back.
To whom do we lay the blame?
Gone.
And so, we live on, holding
her memories like a carton
of eggs as we thumb through

the photographs and play
with her children's children
she'd be desperate to hold.

SQUARE PEGS

We thought we checked
all the boxes:
both love dogs—check
both love fettuccine—check
hard pass on leopard prints—check,
but we didn't know such a thin veneer
        would eventually crack
beneath the weight of overdue bills,
a sink that wouldn't stop leaking,
night shifts and day shifts—us,
two ships passing in the night.
We didn't even buy a dog
or eat fettuccine that much,
and I swear I almost bought leopard
leggings the other day, just for spite.
Honesty, I don't know how to stop the leak,
not in the sink, not in us.
I twirl in the twine of this slow unraveling,
grasping at frayed edges,
still trying desperately to fit
the square of you into the round of me.

TRUTH BE TOLD

*"You will never really see how toxic someone is
until you breathe fresher air." ~Unknown*

Truth be told,
you fancy yourself
a do-gooder,
but there must
be a parade,
with a marching band,
cymbals clashing,
spectators watching
the good you do.

Truth be told,
you adore
the blame-game,
sweeping up guilt
into a dustpan
dumping it at the feet
of those at fault,
absolving yourself
of responsibility.

Truth be told,
you wrap up tightly
in self-pity,
weighted blankets
designed to keep in

the heat of misery,
an outward
demonstration
of practiced piety.

Truth be told,
you keep fastidious
records of wrongs,
forever the meticulous
accountant,
pouring over the books,
ticking tally marks
beside each scorned name,
checking for accuracy.

Truth be told,
Alice,
it would take a team
of highly trained
professionals
to grab your ankles
and drag you away
from your coveted
        looking glass.

UNTETHERED

If we are not tied to one another,
if we have no one who's got our back,

if there's no one to call with good news,
no one to hand us tissues when we cry,

no one to tell us everything will be OK,
no one to lean on when we fail to stand—

then will we just float into the atmosphere,
an untethered balloon without purpose,

drifting across continents, imaging the lives
of the tiny people traveling to and fro?

Will we ride the current of whimsy winds
until our air has seeped away, allowing us

to sink, to succumb to gravity, and there
we will lie, spent, on earth's brown crust?

WATER FRESH AND SALT

Who knew such a roaring flame
could perch atop a micro tongue;

yours was a scorched-earth policy—
leaving nothing behind in its wake,

where even bare-boned promises
were reduced to indeterminant dust,

the kind of scant evidence that makes
forensics clammy with nightmare sweat.

I never understood the enigma presented
in the book of *James* until the sugar-coated

scent of you began to ripen into acrid stench,
until I had to mince around on tip-toe feet,

as to not undermine your egg-shell ego—
then the ancient wisdom words made sense,

*Can both fresh water and salt water flow
from the same spring?*

No. But you defied science and wore anomaly
tucked like a pocket square in a well-tailored suit.

WE OPENED A JOINT ACCOUNT

I do opened up our joint account;
we gave it all we had,
a lifetime of love the set amount;
we knew of nothing bad.

We argued on the playing field;
words became a game;
the house we had begun to build
was little more than frame.

Deposits soon became withdrawals
more going out than in;
we excelled at building walls;
our patience worn and thin.

Our account now sits overdrawn;
we are in the red;
I love you only plays in songs;
we've left those words unsaid.

WHAT LIES BENEATH

The shovel scrapes away
the first layer of dirt,
not much to see there,
just a pebble or two—
things that hint of secrets
yet to be revealed,
but as it bites through
the darker soil,
cutting the underbelly
of lies   and
heaving it upwards,
truth is fully undressed,
          naked
in the menagerie of roots,
in the wriggling body
of a sleepy earthworm—
rain-damp earth still clings
to the edges,
but truth is unmistakable,
is it not?
And the uncovering
only took
a little muscle
and a blade of steel.

YOU WORE RELIGION

You wore religion
like a Sunday suit,
loose and easily
      discardable.
Your prayer tie
hung around your neck,
double-Windsor was it?
Too tight for both of us.
How often did we eat
tossed arguments
topped with low-cal spite?
You looked holy
sitting erect in the pew,
but on Mondays
yesterday's communion
was nothing but memory
on the back of your tongue.

PART III

Low Battery

AREN'T WE ALL A LITTLE BIT MAD?

Whispered voices in my head,
you're not enough.

Those shadows looming long,
silhouettes on cold brick walls,

who's there? My blood runs cold.
Lost inside to-do lists; I can't see

the forest for the trees; running
in circles, a dog chasing its tail.

A fragmented soul is fighting
for composure. She's wafer-thin,

living on caffeine and moments
of clarity in that sliver of space

between wake and sleep.

BETWEEN

thin sliver of time
between wake and sleep
where muses sing,
melody rests on fingers
like iridescent
bubbles, fragile—
temporary,
and it's there,
in that moment
between roundness
and bursting
that a writer must write,
a painter paint,
a musician compose,
for once the between
slips into the deep,
and eyelids close,
creativity sleeps,
the muses become mute,
memories forgotten.

DID I SLEEP

Did I sleep at all last night?
Or did my feet walk that same
tired path
back and forth
back and forth,
wearing out the carpet
of my mind?
Did I wrestle with my worries:
how are the kids,
do they need me,
did I hear a noise,
why is the dog coughing,
why is it 2 a.m.?
Was that me,
carry bricks from one corner
to the other
then carrying those same bricks
back again?
When the sun slit the blinds
like a letter opener,
were my eyes already open
wondering why
I couldn't sleep?

DRIVING BLINDFOLDED

That moment when you look
at the nurse in horror
when she hands you an infant
no bigger than a loaf of bread
and tells you you're going home.
You cry, you beg her to let you stay
there among the professionals,
those consummate experts in baby care.
But she shushes you and says
you'll be just fine; it's all instinct.
Except it isn't, and you freak out
when she cries for no reason,
when your breasts leak milk
and hurt like a mother,
and you don't remember the last time
you slept or what you ate for dinner,
and hours blur into days into weeks—
then suddenly you emerge from the fog
and take a shower, a real shower
that lasts more than thirty seconds,
and you put on real clothes
that don't smell like vomit or poop
(for now).
You breathe in the powder scent of baby,
who, in a dreamless sleep,
looks like the pinnacle of your success.

EMPTY

I finally threw out
the empty carton of energy;

it had expired two years ago
anyway.

Perhaps someday I'll get
another one,

but I'm too tired right now.

FRESH OUT

I'm fresh out of tears,
fresh out of patience
waiting for the change
you said you'd make.
I'm fresh out of hope,
fresh out of apologies
groveling for mistakes
that weren't mine.
I'm fresh out of love,
fresh out of ideas
for how to spin straw
into gold.
I'm fresh out of faith,
fresh out of time;
I'm empty;
get out.

GALAXIES

Oh, to float, weightless,
space embracing my body,
flakes of stardust brushing
the contours of my face,

strands of galaxies winding
like silk around my limbs,
feathers of silence sweeping
away waste and weariness,

the crush of crowds, loud
voices, heavy choices, what's
for dinner, do I have to choose?
Oh, to lose weight, for a moment,

And float.

HITCHHIKING TO THE STARS

Thumb out, walking backwards
feet steady near the ditch,

hoping for a rocket
need a quick escape,

mapped out in light years,
nothing but a backpack,

leaving weight behind.

Can I get a countdown,
systems checked and ready.

I'll wave to the moon
on my way to the stars;

if you see a new light,
sitting in the dipper

you'll know I've arrived.

IMAGINING A SLOW DOWN

What would it look like—
to slow down,
to take my time,
to resist looking at clocks?
What would it be like,
to stretch like a cat in bed,
to wiggle my toes and yawn,
to pad downstairs in my pajamas
and eat toast with jelly
or an omelet with cheese?
What would it be like to read a book,
a whole, delicious book,
one page at a time,
as if I had all the time in the world,
as if nothing and no one pulled
at my shirt, my hair, my attention.
What would it be like to sit in the grass
and listen to doves cooing like lovers,
as if laundry and lists didn't exist?
Would I—if I could—just sit?
Just breathe?
Just be?

LEFT HANGING

The bird feeders hang
                    empty,
the last of the seeds
picked clean
by the most hopeful birds,
the ones who strive
for something
when there's nothing.
I feel wretched
about the emptiness,
really I do,
but yet, I can't work up
the energy
it takes to refill them.
It's February—that awful
month of not quite winter
but quite winter still,
when there's a pallid grayness
in sky, branches and ground.
I open the door
and shout to the birds,
promising to fill
their bellies,
but they don't seem to mind
nearly as much as I,
as they always keep
the promise of spring
tucked beneath their wings.

LORD I'M TIRED

my body's weak,
like cardboard left in rain;
I know you know how much I ache;
I know you've felt my pain.
When it's time to lay me down,
and I've done all that I can do;
hold my hand as I cross the bridge,
and take me home with you.

THE RAZOR'S EDGE

I think I can balance here
in this fragile space
between nodding off
and eyes-wide-open,
but caffeine has waned,
and my body folds
like an ancient accordion,
its ghostly music clashing
with twelve blunt chimes
of the midnight clock.
How many sun-ups
can I endure, exhausted
before the day begins?
My shadow grows thin;
shall I pencil it in—
give shape to spaces
now hollowed out
by little drudgeries?
There's no safe way
to leave this ledge;
a foot slipped
makes the deepest cut.

REDIAL

I'm sorry, the life you have dialed
is unavailable. Please hang up
and try your call again later.

I sigh and go back to laundry,
dirty diapers, a toddler clinging
to my leg for a third snack.

I call again—Wait! Listen! I say
to the recording. I need a beach,
a few good books, sunshine

and seagulls. I'm not asking
for much, just a couple of weeks
—or six, food and drinks included.

I'm sorry, the life you have dialed
is unavailable. Please hang up. . .
I press end and sink into a chair.

TODAY

I want to wrap myself,
in solitude,
to have no other molecules
float in the same space
with my molecules,
to answer no questions,
especially not what's for dinner.
Today I don't want to speak
or hear voices or sounds;
I want to breathe in and out,
to curl up on the couch,
doze off while reading—
or jump in my car and go
where ever I want,
for as long as I want
without demands,
the hundred different things
that consume every waking minute
of every day.
Today I'm tired. Spent. Washed up.
Maybe tomorrow I'll be dancing
with bangles on my wrists
and making chicken casseroles,
but today
I want to wrap myself
in solitude.

WHAT THE WORLD SEES

It's all there,
isn't it?
Splayed out
on social media,
the whole enchilada,
keeping up with the Joneses!
Beach shots,
mountain shots,
fountains in Rome!
Plates of artfully arranged food,
perfectly groomed dogs,
perfectly coifed kids,
picturesque smiles
and positive attitudes.
Heaven forbid
one should post
an ugly cry,
bruises inside,
shadows under eyes,
macaroni and cheese
eaten in plastic bowls
in front of the TV,
laundry piled on the floor,
meltdowns,
breakdowns,
little pills in the drawer
you take for depression
because sometimes

life is just too damn hard
and you can barely
force yourself out of bed
let alone make cute pancakes
to post on Instagram.

PART IV

As the Days Go By

AGING: NOT FOR THE FAINT OF HEART

Weighted down
by rocks of worry,
frown lines creasing
my tissue-thin skin,
feet scuffing
the pavement;
carry on, they say
chin up, they say,
but they don't see
a frame that's cracking,
eaten by moths of time
turning to dust
beneath an ancient sun.

CARRY THE WISH SEED

My grandma was small,
size 4 ½ shoe,
a collector of eagles
(not the living kind);
she talked about Jesus
like she knew him
because she did,
but she had a bit
of whimsy in her, too.
When I was growing up
she'd tell me to carry
a wish seed
anytime I felt anxious
or worried or scared;
so, I did—to tough exams,
to get my driver's license,
to my first job interview,
the day I got married,
the day I got unmarried.
Even decades later,
I store away wish seeds
in the heat of summer,
those tiny white tufts
tucked in my pockets
just in case.

CHURCH CAMPGROUND REUNION

To return to your childhood stomping grounds
    is like looking in a rearview mirror;
each object is the same, yet smaller—and slightly
    out of focus.
You squint into the trees and inhale the familiar
    scent of cedar.
The girls' dorm still stands, white paint chipping off
    old cement blocks,
and you shiver slightly in the goosebump breeze,
    remembering the night
a group of prayer warriors had to cast a demon out
    of a poor girl's soul,
remembering the night you got your period and
    thought you had cancer.
You turn to stare at the long, low building where
    the meetings were held,
each one signaled by the ringing of a brass bell
    that made you come running.
Brown legs pumping, gray gravel skittering in
    all directions;
you dared not be late for the hallelujah courses
    and hell-fire sermons.
The best services were held outdoors in the brush
    harbor—thick poles
stuck into the ground with a roof made from
    branches and brush.
Even mosquitoes made their way to the altar,
    buzzing past your ears.

You were certain the woods held spirits, as you
      made your way down
to the water hole (a trail that felt like two miles—
      but now is only a quarter),
and you wanted to get baptized before the devil
      punched your ticket.
So, the men folk killed three copperheads before
      you waded out,
and the preacher dunked you under water so dark
      you couldn't see your feet.
But you came up to the sound of "Shall We Gather
      at the River,"
and you felt clean enough to be counted
      among the Saints.
There are no baptisms today, and you smell the decay
      that comes from rotting wood
and leaves lain-too-long. Twigs snap in sanctuary shadows,
      and you silently salute the ghost
         of your twelve-year-old self.

THE DECLINE OF OLD DETROIT

How we loved
that cute little house on the hill,
the one with flower boxes filled
with hope and a proud front door,
the color of a robin's egg,
but new things become old
even in the best of times,
and weeds have a way of sprouting
around the edges of manicured lawns,
pushing through cracks in the sidewalks.
We saw the drought coming—
a few bare places in the packed dirt
at the end of a prosperous summer,
a couple factories closing here and there,
some sailing across the foreign sea.
Then, even the weeds turned brown,
and faded paint began to peel;
the house settled into a pout,
making it to where you had to use your hip
to slam the graying front door.
We might have left like the others,
but the '47 Chevy wouldn't start no more
and became lawn art with blocks for wheels.
Air conditioner broke too,
and we moved our couch onto the porch,
where we sat fanning and drinking iced tea.

THE EDGE OF REMEMBERING

Someone once asked me what it was like
to lose my mind; I kid you not, those were
her exact words. She wasn't unkind, just
curious. So, I wrote it down in case she,
or anyone else, ever asked me again,
as I'm sure I won't remember my answer.

Losing your mind is like walking
on the edge of a cliff; the gravel is loose,
you are not wearing proper shoes.
Your foot slips over the side;
you start to fall but catch yourself.

It's nothing, really. Forgetting a wallet.
Losing your car in the grocery parking lot.

You keep walking; the path gets more
narrow, until there really is no path;
your heart pounds as each step teeters
on the edge. You slip again; this time
you go over, rocks scraping your body.

Someone is standing in front of you,
but you can't remember his name.
You left a pan on the stove. It's black.

You manage to catch hold of a branch,
and you cling to it with your bare hands.

92

Your arms begin to shake with the effort,
but you don't want to let go. Then you
are free falling; there's no bottom.

*Strangers around you talk of good days
and bad days. Someone sets boiled eggs
in front of you. You don't know if you like
eggs. You pick at them and remember
a dog you had when you were seven; his
name was Frisco.*

FORGIVE ME IF

I stare out the window too long,
captivated by a honeybee perched
on the velvet-soft lips of a petal.

Forgive me if
I walk into a room and forget
why I'm there. Allow me a wander
to regain my sensibilities.

Forgive me if
I leave the stove on, boil the kettle
dry, burn the toast and serve it dry.
Would you like milk with that?

Forgive me if
I know the name of my first teacher
but don't recognize the contours
of your woeful face today.

Forgive me if
my hands sit idly in my lap,
and I look at them as though they
belong on someone else's arms.

Forgive me if
I slip away without saying goodbye;
I never meant to leave you
with an empty shell.

GRANDMA'S SUNDAY KITCHEN

It was a family affair,
every Sunday in a kitchen
barely big enough for three,
let alone twelve,
but we managed;
tortillas sizzled in skillets
filled with cooking oil,
ground beef simmered
on the next burner over;
it was my job to grate blocks
of cheese, best job ever,
as I could sneak a few strands
to stave off the wild hunger
I'd acquired when Grandpa's
sermon stretched too long.
One aunt was on lettuce duty;
she could slice it paper thin;
another aunt put refried beans
inside the golden shells
(she was the ex-wife of an uncle,
but no one seemed to mind).
When I didn't think I could survive
another minute, the oven would beep,
Mom would pull out pans of burritos
and red enchiladas thick with sauce.
We'd pass the plates and say the prayer
God bless us all; dig in!

HOW TO ANTI-AGE GRACEFULLY

She drove a Jeep
the color of a ripe watermelon
just split open and scraped
from the rind.
Her back was ramrod straight,
fortified with calcium.
Her hair didn't have an ounce
of gray that a salon
couldn't cover with amber brown.
She spent her mornings
on the beach collecting shells
for no other reason
than the search for beauty.
She wore t-shirts and shorts,
bracelets and rings
because she always had—
and still could.
She ate tacos for lunch,
drank tea late into the afternoon,
not worried about caffeine
keeping her awake.
She slept when she wanted,
wrote poetry
in the wee hours of the morning.
She wore age like a silk scarf
trailing in the wind.

LIFE DEFINED

Life lies in valleys
of creased cheeks,
curves along the spine
of a once-straight back,
rolls over knuckles
somehow still able
to bake a loaf of bread.
Life peers through eyes
that have beheld
a dozen babies born,
too many caskets
lowered in the ground.
Life pens
a kaleidoscope of stories,
a memoir for the ages,
        not a fairy tale
but truth-bound pages
scribbled disappointments,
joy inked in margins,
some dreams fulfilled,
others laid to waste.

THE LOVELY JANITOR

Shoulders stooped,
probably from years
of leaning over mop buckets,
white beard resting like snow
on a care-worn ebony face;
he was the gentle sort,
unobtrusive yet kind,
a part of my daily routine,
as I often stayed quite late
at the office.
"Evening, Miss Clara,"
he would say,
pausing for a moment
outside my office door.
I would stop reading and smile,
"Evening, Mr. Otis."
We'd talk about his wife,
his kids, his grandkids,
his bulldog named Buster
as he moved about the room,
cleaning with a silent swish, swish
of a rag, a broom.
The musical cadence in his voice
was like balm to my cracked soul.
When his heart failed him,
I cried for days
and spent evenings staring at my desk,
waiting for the sound of his footsteps,

waiting to hear the soft humming
of *Amazing Grace.*
But he was gone,
and I was a puzzle
with a missing piece.

NOSTALGIA FOR NOSTALGIA'S SAKE

Remember when we slathered ourselves
in baby oil and rolled up our shorts to compare
tan lines and never thought about melanoma?
The sun wasn't that hot back then, was it?
Remember when we thought we knew stuff,
but we really knew nothing at all—except how
to skate backwards and make jars of sun tea.

Remember when dysfunctional was a thing,
but not defined—and no one ever mentioned
suppressed memories because, well, they were
suppressed. Our only counselors were a couple
of ladies in the front office of the school who
peered over their cat eye glasses and smelled
faintly of cigarettes and wintergreen mints.

Remember when the only thing we knew about
politics is that we didn't want to be president
because, historically, some of them got shot,
and we didn't want to be anyone famous either,
as they tended to suffer the same malady—or
ended up married six times and had a thing for
cocaine, but, man, some of them sure could sing!

Remember when we heard our grandpas talking
about the good old days, and we wondered why
our days weren't that good—then we grew up
and talked to our grandkids about the good old

days even though we had battle scars inside and
out—even though we still kept a little dysfunction
tucked away in the closet in a keepsake's box.

WHAT DID YOU DO WITH THE DASH?

When it's over,
when the headstone bears your name
and those two dates with a dash,
the only thing that matters is
  what did you do with the dash?
Did you splash in puddles
with polka dot rainboots?
Dance in your living room?
Make cookies at Christmas?
Did you hold the door open
for the elderly man with a cane?
Did you remember to love,
stare at the constellations,
make a wish on an eyelash?
Did you light a candle,
say a prayer?
Did you relish childhood
like an ice cream that only lasts so long?
Did you create something out of nothing?
Did you keep your nose to the grindstone?
Did you plant daffodils?
Take the trip of a lifetime?
Did you drop a coin in the beggar's box?
Did you learn from mistakes,
live with regrets,
throw away excess baggage?
Did you forgive?
Forget?

Draw a line in the sand?
The dash—

    what did you do with the dash?

WHEN I GROW OLD

will I fall asleep at 7 p.m.?
eat lumpy oatmeal for breakfast?
wear knit sweaters too large for my frame?
send get-well cards to those sicker than I?
will my hair be gray like a river rock
or white like fresh-fallen snow?
I'd prefer white.
will my voice crack when I sing hymns?
will I finally learn how to knit?
will I tell small children to get off my lawn?
will crows' feet track my face?
will I resemble a walking question mark?

YOU CAN'T TAKE IT WITH YOU

Dead.
Deceased.
Passed away.
You're gone,
lying in a box
six-feet under.
Without money,
your house, your metronome.
You can't take it with you.
But what can you leave behind?
Seeds in your garden that will bloom,
daisies, sunflowers, asters, cosmos.
Light in your children's eyes,
living flames of your legacy.
Kind deeds nestled in the eaves
of people's hearts.
Words bled from the end of your pen,
everlasting art.

PART V

The Bigger World

ACTIONS SPEAK LOUDER

What if no one could speak
from the mouth,
and, just for a moment,
the entire world
would rotate on actions?
How do you *act*
I care about the planet?
I help the needy?
I am a good neighbor?
I love my family?
I am a child of God?
Lips sealed,
the silence would spill
our deeds across the earth,
richly soiled with hands
extending compassion
and dignity for all.

CHASING THE UNICORN

The smoke of pretense
thickens the air;
the smell of hypocrisy
so acrid one can taste it
on one's tongue.
Some cry *the children*
others cry *the crime*,
others cry just to hear
the sound of their own
elated voices.
Promises are held in sieves,
draining into useless streams
of imagined utopias.
We must do better, they say;
yet better is merely a unicorn,
forever hidden in the forests
of man's arrogance and greed,
a wishful fairy tale,
the fragments of a dream.

CIVILIZATION
(*dedicated to Ukrainian survivors*)

There's a choking thickness
in the air—gray ash that coats
      throats and memories.
People stoop, even the youngest
appearing ancient—faces gaunt,
hands clutching carrots scattered
      among the cadavers.
Bellies hollow, filled with nothing
but bile for days—eyes transfixed
as they watch dogs gnaw on the
      dead, the half-dead feed on dogs.
There sits the back of a chair, books
with splayed spines, their pages swept
away by the wind, cutlery, teacups,
      a cellphone—all signs of civilization
and yet people are digging through
the dirt, scraping survival from beneath
cinder blocks with broken fingernails,
      unable to process the marquee to
the movie theatre that now sits askew
or the fragmented walls where artwork
once graced a gallery;
      for not a single soul can bake *Atlantis* or
boil a Vasyl Krychevsky in the aftermath of
an aggressor who slashes sovereignty as though
he is some primeval predator who has never held
      a wine glass in his claws.

We've come so far, people say—and yet
it is achingly obvious we have not come
far enough.

CORNER OF FIFTH AND MAIN

I see her a lot, the woman on the corner;
Sometimes she looks young: long pig tails,
fishnet stockings and lipstick the color
of a pink peony—other times I see the years
in the curve of her shoulders as she lights
a cigarette or the way she rests her back
against the lamppost. Once, when I drove by,
our eyes met—and there was a brief flicker
of something behind her ice-blue gaze,
a kind of longing maybe, or perhaps anger.
I'd like to know how she got there,
but I can't very well stop and ask—can I?
Excuse me, ma'am, where are you from?
Did your dreams-on-fire turn into ashes
—who are you; who do you want to be?
I've made up my mind; I will stop today.
But today there are red and blue lights,
police tape, and a sheet-covered body
on the ground.

COUNT THE SECONDS,
DIVIDE BY FIVE

It thunders like a standing ovation.
After the last note hangs in the air,
after the actors take one last bow,
carnations and success clutched
to their happy, heaving chests.
It thunders like wild horses
galloping through a canyon,
manes flowing, earth tone bodies,
bits and bridles as foreign as baboons.
It thunders like a toddler's tantrum,
splayed face-down on the floor,
arms and legs flailing windmills.
It thunders like a preacher
under a billowing white tent,
mopping his brow, voice raised
to a hell-fire fever pitch, still strong
on night five of a week-long revival.
It thunders like two drunks in a bar,
each thinking he's the biggest rooster,
neither worth a plugged nickel on Sunday;
they reek of whiskey and regret.
It thunders like food poisoning after sushi
that tasted a little off. It thunders like two
elephants learning the tango, all left feet.
It thunders like an oil-slicked alley
full of shadows, tin cans, and needles.
It thunders like apologies left unsaid.

CRACKS IN HUMANITY

crumbled bricks, trash whirling
like tumbleweeds down deserted streets,
jobs lost,
shutters hanging from homes
long abandoned
after the last pill of hope
fell down the drain,
factories moved
to foreign soil,
people left behind
to scratch life out of dirt
like chickens in the yard,
prices up, bridges down,
who's at fault
for the fault lines?
Who can drink enough sorrow
to irrigate the earth?

DECAY

black headlines
covered with smoke and debris,
how many have fallen today?
those pretty places
with flowers on the table,
white coffee cups with handles,
now in disarray
petals scattered across still forms,
cups shattered into pieces;
these are not genteel times,
though they could be—
had respect not slipped out
the back door,
carrying compassion on its back,
had isolation not driven
each into his own corridor
of madness and depravity;
can we even put a finger
on who's to blame for the anger,
who first let slip
through their fingers
the essence of all that it means
to be human?

A DIFFERENT KIND OF HUNGER

Jazz notes spill out onto the sidewalk
with well-heeled patrons in leathers
and tweeds, denims, and cashmeres.
A rift cut in half by the closing door,
laughter fades in the damp-drizzle
night as rosy-faced desirables
make their way to the next club.
I'm sure they didn't notice the man
sitting just outside the door, but had
they opened the door a fraction wider,
it would have hit him—would have
bruised his sign that said *Will Work for
Food*, would have bruised his ego,
had he had one left. There's an empty
wrapper near his shoeless foot; will it
sustain the hunger that turned his ribs
into shadows?

EXPENDABLES

when shadows
become monsters,
when safe spaces
are blown away
like a house of cards,
when hate
turns the world
inside out
and shakes it
by its teeth,
when human life
is expendable,
blanks in the mind
of the deranged.

FROM A FORMER SKELETON

Nights were the hardest in Auschwitz;
that's when hunger would gnaw
at your belly like rats on bare toes,

when you knew your next meal was at least
six hours away—a gruel so thin it was little more
than rain water with a chunk of stale bread.

Nights—that's when we did the most dreaming,
not the sleep dreaming, but the eyes-wide-open
nostalgia for our homes, our Shabbat, our food—

Imagine this, someone would whisper, *slow-roasted*
brisket, brown juices spreading across the plate
when your fork sinks deep inside the tender meat.

Ah, yes, someone else would reply, *can you smell*
the chocolate babka! Look, I'm tearing off a piece,
chewing; the bread is nearly melting in my mouth.

A soft laugh from a lower bunk then, *Cholent—*
Bubbe seasoned the beef, potatoes, and carrots
just right; it was fit for a king, I tell you! On and on

we'd go like this, each of us recalling family recipes.
Eventually, we'd fall silent, lost in a different time—
before mad men turned meat into bones.

GENETICS

What shall come tumbling out
of this baby lying still in my lap
sucking his thumb? What inner
workings lie within his mind,
dormant, yet maybe just so,
until a crest of late blooming
as he sprouts into toddler, child
and teen. Raking through leaves
of his past, (heritage, the agency
calls it) will those discoveries
come trumpeting into his life
like a herd of pissed elephants?
Will they scream and throw things;
will they require the steady hands
of professionals and saints?
Will the trail of cocaine use,
malfunctions, disorders. . .
you know,
that one maternal grandmother,
that crazy uncle—somehow mar
this still-cradled soul,
or can nurture overcome
those ancient natured beasts?

LEFT FIELD

He's smaller than most fifth-graders. Clings to the chain-link fence, watching me coach little league. His jeans torn, sneakers a grayish-white. He mimics the players on the field, pretending to throw or catch, although he has neither mitt nor ball. He doesn't belong to any of the parents I know, and he always disappears before the end of the game—except the day he doesn't. As I put away the bats, I startle to find him standing near the dugout. "Can I hit once?" he asks, swiping a fringe of dirty blond hair off his forehead. I notice a small cut above his eyebrow. "Uh, sure," I say. I hand him a bat and go to the mound. He swings at the first pitch—too late. The next pitch, the same. He steps closer to the plate and adjusts the bat. On the third pitch, the crack echoes across the park. I watch the ball sail above over my head, beyond the fence. I turn around, ready to congratulate him, but he's gone.

endless sky
the scoreboard still
zero to one

LESSONS FROM MRS. P

I'm staring out the windows of PS104,
crisscrossed by irons bars;
ain't much different than prison,
least that's what my uncle says;
he's been in both.
I would like to know adverbs,
make friends with them on paper,
really, Mrs. P, I would,
but my eyes won't stay open.
Romero got shot last night,
just outside another set of barred
windows—you know the ones,
Mrs. P, that gas station on 48th?
Or maybe you don't go to that one.
Bet that's why you like adverbs,
cause you use the east side gas,
and maybe I'd like them, too, but I'm
too busy watching my back—
and my front, too, truth be told.
My little sister ain't doing so good
after Mom's shit boyfriend laid hands
on her; know what I mean Mrs. P?
So, nothing personal when I leave
this page blank; survival has a way
of making words blur together,
all funny like. I might still get it though;
I'll let you know if I ever defend myself
gallantly. See what I did there Mrs. P?

LISTENING

I sit, watching a deaf couple sign;
no sound is needed,
just faces and hands.
I can't understand the conversation,
but I can gauge the mood,
based on body language alone,
and I find myself smiling when they smile,
leaning forward with excitement
when they lean forward.
And I wonder, what if we were all deaf?
What if we had to look at each other
with new eyes?
What if words poured from the ends
of our fingers,
and every story we told
ebbed and flowed with our bodies?
What if we listened
with our hearts?

MELTING DOWN

One-hundred degrees in the shade,
not a cliché, just God's-honest truth,
the kind of summer made for kids
and water hoses and those kind of popsicles
you suck out of long plastic tubes,
dribbling red juice down your chin.
But it wasn't the kind of summer made for parents
with too little money and too many bills,
pent up in a house reeking of cigarettes and sorrow,
the A/C on its last leg, sputtering out semi-warm air
from its place on the paint-chipped window sill.
Funny how heat and humidity and hatred
create the perfect storm,
a storm filled with lightning and the distant rumble
of thunder, but without a drop of rain in sight,
the flash of a fist,
the crash of a plate;
no one cries—
a nearly-grown girl lies on top of her mattress,
waiting for the leaves to change
and the first snowflake of winter.

MOUTHS IN MOTION

Well-rehearsed lies are the best,
the kind that roll easily off the tongue,
iridescent oil refracted by spotlights,
showcased in suits and power ties,
blazers and skirts—spoken from podiums
adorned with compliant media mics.
How do they look so composed,
these politicians full of promises
and platitudes? There must be a school
somewhere in the back halls of Congress,
an acting school, a Hollywood spin-off,
with large mirrors, stages, voice coaches.
We're not supposed to peek behind the curtain
—which is why most of us watch from our TVs.
See the mouths move? See how their words
transform lives? How they clean up our streets,
reduce crime, keep us out of another recession?
No. I don't suppose you do. Neither do I.
We've been duped, you and I—we've listened
to humans pretending to be gods and never saw
Mount Olympus burning to the ground.

NO COMMON GROUND

Left of center;
Right of center;
neither side will lay down arms.
Rhetoric shot through the heart;
can't see anything for the smoke.
Civility, long deceased,
and unity—the intangible ghost.
No one can hear one another
above the pandemonium,
each willing to die
on his self-righteous sword
for the sake of a grievance,
real or perceived.
Let's roll out the red carpet
for lab-grown victimhood;
let's crown the victors
of division
who have tossed the Molotov
and reduced a nation's hope
to ashes.

ORIGAMI

So many bodies.
Bodies stink;
bodies move.
I don't want
to be a body
in this body,
the education
population.
If I could,
I would fold myself
into a paper crane
and fly across
the campus,
free of lockers
and sweaty arms
bumping into mine,
free from the clamor
that jackhammers my brain,
free from the teachers
who look to me for answers
when I have none.
I cross my thin arms
over my chest,
hold my books
like a breastplate;
I shrink into seats,
making myself
as small as possible.

But I'm not small enough.
I don't have enough folds;
no one gave me wings.

RABBIT

I recognized the hunch of your thin shoulders,
the way your eyes skittered back and forth
as he cursed at you in the Walmart parking lot.
He wanted to make sure everyone heard
his clever use of the F word, tough *man*
in his wife beater and camouflage shorts.
Trust me honey, I know his type.
I couldn't help but watch you in the aisles,
darting first this way than that, a rabbit
attempting to escape her predator,
yet knowing there's no way out.
You were looking for an item; an employee
and I tried to help—but we heard him yelling
at you again near the front of the store.
Perhaps you weren't quick enough, rabbit.
It broke my heart to see you hop like that.
We exited together, and I watched you
push the heavy cart across the parking lot,
the wheels veering awkwardly over bumps,
while he walked behind you
swinging his empty arms.
I wanted to say something to him, rabbit.
I wanted to give him a piece of my mind;
I wanted to give *you* a piece of my spine
that allowed me to walk away years ago.
Promise me you'll fight, dear rabbit—
there's a better life outside the burrow.

SILENCER

My shoulder bumps into another shoulder
in the crosswalk, but neither of us says sorry,

or maybe we do mumble something, at least
in our heads. What does it matter in the sludge

of humanity, heads bowed to the mobile gods,
bowed against bitterness, bowed with intent

towards a thousand destinations. My lashes
feel wet, but I know I'm not crying. No one

has time for salt; so, I raise my face to the sky,
and there they are—luminescent white flakes

cascading from the sky, as though the one God
who *should* exist has shaken a feather pillow

from heaven's bed, and I stop, just inches
from the sidewalk, face upturned, receiving cold

baptisms, until someone clips my arm with his
backpack and mutters something about getting

killed by a taxi. I move, but only to the safety
of the curb then tuck myself back just a foot

or so from bodies pressing forward, oblivious
to miracles nesting in hair, framing footprints,

softening the sharp elbows of the city, muting
its cacophony of curses and catastrophes.

I stand motionless, as if inside a globe shaken
by a gleeful toddler, stand until I cannot feel

my hands, my feet. Stand until there is nothing,
no one, until I am the sole survivor in the city's
anti-apocalypse.

THE SOUND OF SILENCE

mouths—tight-closed slashes,
heads down, brows furrowed
as if the weight of the world
lies inside a screen of apps,
as if the answers lie there, too;
feet stumble across pavement,
shoulders bump without apology,
each burrowed in his faux sense
of progress and pride;
ah, the fooling of fools,
those who believe they're in touch,
yet they touch nothing, no one;
　　　　they seek
information without knowledge,
have friends they wouldn't know
if they kissed them in the streets,
calendars full of appointments,
hamsters on wheels;
even when their mouths move,
they say nothing; abject silence covers
screams; blanched of human decency,
they float like ghosts in search of Wi-Fi.

STAINED GLASS PRAYERS

Something draws me inside
St. Patrick's Cathedral,
and I tell myself it's the architect,
but the moment I pass through
the grandiose, arched doors,
and the chaos of the city fades
like wisps of smoke into air,
I know there is something more.
There are candles on a table,
and I light one, not because I'm
Catholic, but because we share
the same God. I glance to my left;
there's a woman, old and bowed,
resembling a plump question mark.
She lights a candle, too, and I notice
tears streaking her deeply-lined face.
Then she crosses herself and prays.
She doesn't bow her head but looks
straight at the stained-glass windows.
The late afternoon sun pours through
saints, angels, Jesus, and many other
figures I don't recognize. But it's not
the beauty of the light-infused glass
that renders my mannequin stance,
but the woman's face—transformed,
otherworldly, her lines seem to fade,
and the sun surrounds her gray hair,
like a real-life halo. Her lips move,

but I can't make out the words.
I don't need to. She's not speaking
to me. And I don't have the answers.

STATE OF THE HUMAN ADDRESS

We pop our pills and guzzle them down
with fruit infused water from plastic bottles,
which we promptly recycle, but they still
end up surprising sea turtles beyond the bay.
We excuse our behaviors with a myriad
of labels we have so cleverly carved
from the recesses of our minds—it's fine,
we say to the bipolar, narcissistic, manic
depressive—here, have some more pills.
Then go to work in your 9 x 9 cubicle,
stare at a screen, have as little interaction
as possible. But make sure you visit the gym
on your day off. Hamburgers are unhealthy,
but the FDA approved Red Dye 40, in small
amounts, naturally. Drive around pot holes;
the bridges are perfectly safe, as are the trains,
(except in cases of collapse or derailments).
The more you go to concerts, movie theaters
and shopping malls, the better you'll feel—
unless, of course, there's an active shooter.
In that case, run for your lives; it's all random.
You at least have some semblance of control
when you order your tall Frappuccino, extra shot
of espresso, soy milk, no whip cream, light ice,
and sip it through a biodegradable paper straw.
Never settle for silence, not even while pumping
gas; entertainment can maintain equilibrium, but
thinking is unhealthy and may result in unwanted

education, a frightful peek under the bloated belly
of government bureaucracies and overspending.
At some point, you can retire, but not until
your joints have reached optimal arthritis;
that's really the best time to buy a red sports car
and wear those pricey sunglasses you craved
in your twenties. Still unfulfilled? Visit a beach,
say hello to the turtles, pick up rogue plastic,
increase your medication.

WE CAME BACK

War is never over,
but some declare it so.
We shake off the sand
but forever feel the grit
between our teeth.
Some of us stand
like flamingos
on one leg;
others ain't so lucky
and sit like toads
in wheels chairs.
Even those who come back
       intact
leave pieces of themselves
        behind—
the piece that was innocence,
the piece that wished on stars,
the piece that believed in something.
We came back
to sleep in our own beds
but wake up screaming,
sweat soaking our t-shirts,
tears streaming down our faces.

WHEN I GROW UP

It's an ordinary day
in my 5th grade classroom,
relaxed even,
which is as rare as unicorns.

Expecting clever answers,
I ask the kids, one-by-one,
what they want to be
when they grow up:

nurse
teacher (like you Ms. Lake)
pilot
monkey trainer
pizza taster
video game maker
football player. . .

I reach the last child, Leo,
not sure if he will talk;
the thin brown-haired boy
often sits, arms hugging his legs,
his dark eyes wide and wary.

So, Leo, I say, keeping my voice
light,
*what would you like to be
when you grow up?*

Safe, he says.

I sit with his answer
the rest of my life.

THE WORLD IS CANCELLED TODAY

Thunderous noise,
donkeys and elephants
stampeding toward the same cliff;
all bent on mutual self-destruction,
all lost in the applause of their own
precarious feet.
Perhaps the rest of us
should hang back,
gather up our flashlights,
water bottles,
generators,
granola and grape preserves
and wait until the dust settles.

PART VI

Natural Remedies

BEACH MORNINGS

I inhale and exhale,
in sync with the rhythm
of the ocean:
in   out
in   out.
Alone on the beach,
I sit like a statue,
knees to chin,
arms wrapped
around my legs.
The sun has yet
to crest the dunes.
In   out.
I marvel at the life
around me,
crabs sidestepping,
like marionettes
on the strings
of a master puppeteer,
gulls circling overhead,
screeching for French fries
and other bad habits
humans have bestowed
upon the wild.
A wave laps my toes,
and I reach out to fetch

a shell in the shape
of a heart.
In   out.

BREAKTHROUGH

Beneath a slab-gray sky,
lashes wet with icy mist,
I curse the winter claws
still latched on to spring.
It's the linger season—
a bad ex you just can't shake.
I've almost resigned myself
to a six-month prison stint
when I see a daffodil, stiff
and resolute, a canary
in the snow.

LAKE ERIE IN ASHTABULA

Tan sand stretches for miles,
water and sky bump hips
like best friends.
There's a languid peace,
the unhurried search for beach glass,
rocks tumbling ashore like jewels
spilled from a vintage pawn shop.
There's space to spread your arms,
turn, turn, turn;
lose yourself in beautiful simplicity;
wrap yourself in fizzy Zen
as the last rays of sun blush a pink farewell.

LAKE TRIOLET

Do you remember the ripples we made with our toes,
the sun warm on our backs?
We had nowhere to be and nowhere to go.
Do you remember the ripples we made with our toes?
We watched a dragonfly doze
and a heron fish from the edge of the bank.
Do you remember the ripples we made with our toes,
the sun warm on our backs?

LIFE IN THE CRACKS

well-tended gardens,
acres of blooms placed just-so,
aesthetically pleasing;

someone paid big money to
imitate nature's bounty of goods,
blending colors, shapes. . .

like any designer worth
his salt—people will pause, snap
pictures, oohing, ahhing—

but here I crouch,
at a crack in the sidewalk, lens
focused on a single yellow

bloom; some call it
a weed; I call it tenacity, nature's
rebellion against the confines

of man.

OCEAN TRIOLET

We once vacationed by the sandy shores,
so young and full of possible.
Our eyes held stars and love's sweet core.
We once vacationed by the sandy shores.
Our skin turned golden as we explored,
still unlined by time.
We once vacationed by the sandy shores,
so young and full of possible.

PILGRIMAGE

A hush drapes like a prayer shawl over my shoulders the moment my feet step from path to pine needles. I bow my head, an apologetic repentance, *Mother Nature, forgive me; it's been five years since my last confession.* But there's no judgment in the dappled dots of sunlight that filter through the age-old canopy, no condemnation in the trill of the birds. I stop in the middle of the trail, inhaling cedar, oak leaves—the scent of earth recycling herself in the underbrush. Someone watches me with warm, doe eyes but doesn't tell me I don't belong; she simply nods and nudges the leaves. Unexpected tears turn the forest into an abstract painting, swirls of green, amber, gold, and brown. I finally reach the stream I once knew as well as myself. Now I know neither stream nor self, but I allow my fingers the luxury of baptism until they ache with cold and memories.

a leaf swept downstream
my destination unknown

PORCH SUMMERS

skin sticky with sweat,
tasting of salt,
fireflies winking, blinking
in the gathering dusk,
me on my cot,
another animal in the night,
lying on Gram's front porch,
listening to the distant tune
of *Bennie and the Jets*,
and the racoons rummaging
through the trash
for the freshest scraps,
eyes opening, closing
my head growing heavy
beneath a moon
bitten in two
by the mice.

RIVER FOR KEEPS

To wrap the river
around my finger
like a remember string,
to feel its coolness,
to watch rainbow trout
shimmy in the sun,
to sink my toes
in the muddy bank
and mimic the bullfrogs'
quirky quartet—
that would be enough,
I think,
to carry me through
the winter,
this season of short days
and even longer nights,
when my own face
stares back at me
from darkened windowpanes.

THE SELF-MADE POET

counting dimes, living on tortillas
and refried beans, poetry workshops
beyond the hills—
designed for others, not for me;

so, I hung metaphors
in the branches of every tree,
shook punctuation out of stars,
looked an earth worm

in the face—or was it the tail?
I let similes drench my hair,
splashed my boots in imagery,
kept rhythm with the rain;

I squeezed couplets
out of oranges, let the juice
drip down my chin, hung
laundered rhymes on the line;

they smelled like sunshine
and lilacs and unpretentious
adjectives, and I laughed
and laughed and laughed,

amused by the anaphora
that tickled the end of my nose
like a piece of sweet clover
the size of a bunny's tail.

STOPPING IN THE WOODS WITH FROST

My chore: to gather wood that day,
but a bed invited me to stay
beneath the canopy of trees
a mossy sponge of sweet decay.

Dots of sunlight filtered through
where a clump of violets grew;
birds bantered with choral songs,
a resplendent rendezvous.

The breeze blew cobwebs from my mind,
my worries I could cast behind;
a chipmunk paused quite near my face
I could touch him if so inclined.

These woods are rich, green and deep,
but I have promises to keep,
and miles to go before I sleep,
and miles to go before I sleep.

SUMMER TRIOLET

I watch the leaves then close my eyes
in a swing beneath the tree;
the crickets are singing a lullaby.
I watch the leaves then close my eyes;
an indigo brush is painting the sky
deep blue of solitude.
I watch the leaves then close my eyes
in a swing beneath the tree.

UNDER THE CANOPY

My footsteps are cushioned
by fallen leaves, and I inhale
the scent of earth and recycled
life that lies beneath decay.
I'm surrounded by a symphony
that only the woods can make:
branches rustling together like
sandpaper, the trill of a cardinal,
the *skiff skiff* of tiny animal feet.
As I approach the narrow clearing,
I see my throne, the majestic slab
stone with a flat seat and raised
arms, and smile. Nothing
has changed—not the green tint
of moss, not the way
the sun filters through what I called
the Heaven hole when I was a kid,
and I'd lift my arms toward the sky,
allowing the sun to envelope my face.
I sit down and close my eyes, breathe.
How many times had I sat,
tucked away in my own earthy globe,
reading books, writing journals, trying
to understand the mystery of boys
and the ache from rejection.
I had long since moved on. Boys, as it
turns out, were not *that* mysterious, and
rejection only comes when you can't find

a way to love yourself. My throne had
taught me this; I just need to return
once in a while and be queen for a day.

WHEN FOXES PLAY

Oh, how I envy her,
the young mother,
her red fur shining,
a copper penny
in the sun.
Her two kits follow,
two black buttons,
not yet old enough
to don the red.
They bounce as though
their slender legs
have springs inside.
I tap my lame foot
on the patio stones;
      inside I'm leaping,
a kit without a cage.
I almost laugh aloud
when mother dodges
her young one's pounce.
He tumbles, nose first
into the clover.
Oh, how I envy her,
the grinning babes,
the humming bees,
each busy in the season
of their lives
that have yet
to see boundaries.

WRITING MUSES

Sunshine has a smell (so does rain)—not the bottled
kind, but the genuine, hung-out-on-the-line-to-dry
kind (the sky-ripe-with-blue-bruised-clouds kind),

and it's there I like to hang my hat, there my words
catch a ride on the wind, like hopeful wishes blown
from tender weedy stems.

Sunshine is baked into strands of hair, iron-warm
against the head, absorbed into cheeks that blush
beneath the buttered rays.

Rain is earth returned to sky, and sky returned
to earth, baptisms from above, plants' salvation,
respite for sunburnt souls.

So, I sit and write, bare feet on the porch rails,
rain—or shine, it matters not, poems saturated
with both, eyes dry; eyes full of tears.

PART VII

Laughter is the Best Medicine

BEFORE SOCIAL MEDIA

Before people showed pictures of their
sandwiches, before you had to reveal every
thought and feeling, before the meme wars,
before all that misinformation (according to
those who make such judgments), before
adding friends you never knew, before cats
talked and goats wore tutus, before you knew
Susan was pregnant before her husband did,
before you knew tweets didn't come from
birds, before you snap-insta-chatted-grammed
every five minutes, before your phone sprouted
like a tree branch out of your palm, before
headlines were click-bait (and quite untrue),
before you compared your life to Karen's—with
her house and polished children and three-car
garage, before you blocked people with one
click—you happily ate bologna, watched TV
only when men landed on the moon, minded
your own, fed your non-talking cat, had no idea
Susan was pregnant until she was eight-months
along and you ran into her at the grocery store,
birds tweeted in the trees, you snapped beans
and talked over the backyard fence, clutched a
toddler in each hand (completely unpolished),
didn't know a single person named Karen, and
blocked people with the solid slam of your front door.

FAMILY REUNION

Everyone would be there;
so, I decided to skip that year,
skip the half-baked cod
Aunt Bert brings,
skip the triplets,
especially the one
with the left eye that turns
out; never knew which way
she was looking.
It was 1982. E.T. phoned home.
"I Love Rock and Roll" played
on the radio no less than ten
times a day. Aqua Net, a beauty
staple. But I just couldn't do it.
Couldn't watch Uncle Harvey
pick his nose or his third wife,
Nancy, pick through his hair
like a monkey looking for fleas.
So, I went to the Over Easy Café
instead—no picking going on there.
The bacon was crisp to perfection,
sourdough bread golden toasted,
lettuce, tomatoes, & creamy mayo
miles away from that God-awful
plum pudding Gertrude always made.
She wasn't even in our family!
Man, that was a helluva good year
for marvelous mental health.

HATS OFF TO

runners
wearing designer
sports gear
neon tennis shoes
fashionable pony tails

body builders
lifting weights
flexing biceps
all muscle, no fat
chugging milk proteins

bicyclists
adorable helmets
skin-tight pants
body streamlined
traveling 100 miles

me
getting out of bed
chasing a toddler
writing poetry
narrowly avoiding
      mental breakdowns.

I HEARD A FLY BUZZ

Like nails on a chalkboard
or the sound a fork makes
scraping a plate—
a fly buzzes
against the windowpane,
an incessant grating
against the fibers
of my nerves;
I move in,
and we begin
a circular dance
of irregular movements,
fits and starts,
dashes, dodges,
elbows akimbo—
and the fly stays
      just out of reach.
He seems to know
his days, his minutes,
are numbered,
that he will no longer
waggle his wings
or track dots of poop
across my ham on rye;
he stills,
and I wonder if he sees
a thousand of me

just before the perfected
snap of a dish towel
ends his insipid life.

I NAMED HIM PATRICK

The mouse made his way into our garage,
foolish decision, really—trusting humans
to ignore an invading presence,
regardless of size.

His nose should have warned him
about the scent of peanut butter—
a most unnatural occurrence in nature,
especially at the end of a plastic tube.

But, alas, primal hunger overrode
that chill down his spine,
the way the hairs stood at attention
on the back of his thimble neck,

and in he went, more than happy
to gorge on the sticky-sweet paste—
until he turned to seek a drink,
his nose bumping the end of life.

And that's where I found him,
desperate to undo the choices
that had tempered his tiny feet,
held hostage his tickling whiskers.

I should have let him die;
that's what my friends told me to do,
each a human not inclined to abide
the encroachment of a single mouse,

but I couldn't bear to look into eyes
that clearly showed regret and sorrow;
so, I named him Patrick and released him
into the woods near the high school.

He sat on the fallen log for a long moment,
thanking me for his undeserved freedom
then scampered into the underbrush,
vowing to learn from his mistakes.

MEASURING STICK

Oh, to be you—that woman
in produce—with slimming black slacks
and a chiffon blouse, who can simply squeeze
a peach, thump a melon, run a finger over
a clump of grapes and select the finest, freshest
fruit on the shelf. Oh, to clip clop down the aisles
in graceful heels, a glossy mane of gold cascading
down my back. I pause beside you and stare at the
wine display, pretending I, too, must select a bottle
to pair with a rack of lamb and roasted asparagus.
You choose red. I sneak a glance—ah, yes, a fine
Cabernet Sauvignon! I would have chosen the same,
had I not had my heart set on cooking mac and cheese
and hamburgers. Here is where we part ways, I think,
but then I see you again in the checkout line. You've
added a bouquet of baby pink roses and white lilies
to your basket. How novel! I rattle my wanky-wheeled
cart over to the florist and select a clump of half-price,
half-wilting carnations, which will probably be flung
to the floor by two toddlers. And I can't help but wonder
—who will sit at the opposite end of your pricey stems?
A lover? A friend? I sigh but hold my head high as I exit
the store behind you, flip-slops slapping a beat on the
soles of my feet. I bet you wear a size six.

A MEMORIAL SERVICE FOR MEMORY

Oh, Memory, we are gathered here
today to pay tribute to the days
when you were alive and well—
when I could remember where
I put my car keys,
why I walked into a room,
to turn on the crockpot.
I took you for granted, Memory,
and I'm sorry—sorry I didn't
appreciate buying more milk
before we ran out
or paying bills when they were due.
Memory, you served me well for years,
and I guess, somewhere in the back
of my mind, I knew you were fading,
but I didn't know how desperately
I would miss you.
And now—it's too late.
I have no idea where the screwdriver is;
I swear I put it in the drawer just last week.
I wore different colored socks today,
which someone (not you) graciously
pointed out.
May you rest in peace, Memory.
As for me, I cannot rest.
I'm too busy trying to remember.

OUT OF ORDER

must have food,
hours in the waiting room
have left me ravenous;
my stomach is eating itself;
so, I wind my way through seats
and reach the vending machine
(circa 1975).
Five sad bags of plain potato chips,
three chocolate bars,
a package of cookie wafers.
Perhaps the machine has not been stocked
since 1975. No matter, I shove my dollar
into the slot;
the slot spews it back at me,
like a toddler rejecting broccoli.
I smooth the dollar then try again;
It takes the bill.
Let's see, 4D for chocolate.
Nothing.
6E for chips.
Nothing.
8C for cookies.
A light whirring sound;
the cookies hang, suspended,
at the edge of the release ring,
I bang on the front of the machine;
nothing.
Give me my cookies! I shout.

I pound. I grab the side
of that unyielding beast
and shake it for all it's worth.
Then I feel a hand on my shoulder.
One of the clinic staff says gently,
Ma'am this machine is out of order.

THE PROS AND CONS OF LOVE
EXPLAINED IN TWENTY LINES

You are the cotton to my candy,
the caramel to my apple,
the peanut butter to my jelly,
the pepper to my salt,
the dressing to my salad,
the icing to my cake.

You are the thorn to my rose,
the sand in my swimsuit,
the seeds in my watermelon,
the ant at my picnic,
the rain on my parade,
the mosquito in my sleep.

You're the fish that I caught,
and I won't throw you back,
even when you smell like gouda cheese.

You are all that I need
and all that I lack;
you are the tissue when I sneeze,

the bee in my bonnet,
the Halley to my comet.

READ THE SIGN

I don't care if you
gave socks to a homeless guy
or donated books to the library
or invented a strawberry that
can last in the fridge for weeks
without rotting or rode a roller
coaster sixteen times without
throwing up or looked cute in
a black mini skirt even though
you're 55 or caught a fly ball
at the game then had it signed
by the pitcher or attended mass
in St. Paul's Cathedral in Rome
and dropped a coin in the Trevi
Fountain and danced in the rain
near the Spanish steps or served
hotdogs and Coke at the school
concession stand or gave up your
parking spot to a sparkly old lady
who drove a Jeep with the top off
or planted a mango tree in memory
of your Uncle Zeus who never saw
a tree he didn't like or rescued a bag
of unwanted puppies from the river—
you cannot feed the pigeons!

PART VIII

The Way Back

THE ART OF BEING

Eyes closed,
there's a slow melting away,
a laying down of all things
heavy;
I immerse myself in sound
like a warm bubble bath—
the song of a robin,
the distant laughter of a child,
the tinkling of windchimes;
I breathe in;
I breathe out.
The wind carries the scent
of lilacs and honeysuckle,
fresh-cut grass,
and someone's barbeque;
I breathe in;
I breathe out
then open my eyes.
Nothing has changed,
and yet everything has changed.
I am lighter,
floating on top of a cloud
that looks like an elephant.

BEEN A LONG TIME COMING

I shed toxicity like a snake
sheds its skin,
carve out the cancer cells
with the thinnest
steel scalpel and with great
precision.
It's been a long time coming.

I recreate myself, creep out
of that cocoon,
and admire my new wings,
unfold them,
flying from the choking grasp
of timidity.
It's been a long time coming.

I stand tall, like a she warrior
in a hero film,
hands on hips, meaning business,
staring back
at the bridges I intend to burn,
and burn I do.
It's been a long time coming.

Peace envelopes me; feathery
wings of angels
brush the hair from my eyes;
soul music

fills every inch of my being;
I'm at rest.
It's been a long time coming.

FANNING THE FLAMES

Coals left burning,
beneath spent wood
of brittle dreams;
still red,
still hot;
he pokes and pokes,
stirring the ashes,
smirked satisfaction.
He thinks you're done;
he's used every splinter
of you,
except he didn't count
on the winds of change
to breathe life into loss,
to reignite the flames.
He draws back,
the heat too intense,
and you burn down
the citadel.

THE GRAND ESCAPE

She, a great Houdini,
slipped through the knots
that had bound her wrists
more years than she dared
count.

Obscured in a cloud of mist,
she vanished from the stage
and found herself in a foreign
land called liberty;
she breathed.

She wondered, just briefly,
if he'd try to pull her back,
pull a rabbit out of the hat,
so he could saw her in half
again.

But no amount of magic
could coax her body through
the ethereal divide;
she'd planned her exit well,
center stage.

MAKE SPACE

for mistakes,
for those raw imperfections
you often find when looking
through mirrors not your own;
for unabated grief,
for the trauma-fed tears
that stain your pillowcase;
for the jagged pieces
that no longer fit together
but nevertheless make a whole;
for remembering,
for conjuring all the moments
that sparkle like tiaras in the sun;
for second chances,
for those paths you found and forged
while walking through the weeds.

NOT IN MY DNA

useless complaints,
trimming in paint,
making excuses,
things without uses,
keeping a neutral face;
junk and clutter,
a day without butter,
playing fake nice,
paying full price,
panties scratchy with lace;
running for fun,
scorching hot sun,
a fly in the house,
sweat down my blouse,
tears of a drama queen;
people who lack
good manners and tact,
repetitive sounds:
pound, pound, pound, pound,
politics on the big screen.

PATCHED

There's a crack running lengthwise
down the middle of my heart,
in that section where people drive
over and over,
that section that endures both heat
　　　　and ice.
I've patched it over the years,
with arms that love me,
with chin-up self-talks,
with grace from God.
But it's there, beneath the bubbled
asphalt—not quite as smooth
as the original paving.

REMOTE CONTROL

You hold the remote
in your hand;
turn off the news,
agendas screaming
like banty roosters.
Unwind—let the kite
take a journey
on the wind;
float above the fray.
You hold the remote
in your hand;
turn off the voices
inside your head,
those that tell you
you're not enough.
Rise out of the ashes,
Phoenix reborn.
You hold the remote
in your hand;
turn off the drama,
the pokers and pot stirrers.
Use a door
that locks from the inside.
What a satisfying click!
You hold the remote.

SWEEPING

Armed with a broom
and dustpan,
I sweep up the fragments
of my dreams,
dropped because my arms
were too full—
too many unset boundaries
too many times of saying yes
instead of no
too many voices clamoring.
I think I can use super glue,
repurpose the mended
whole;
I'll just need to find that one
missing piece
that skidded under the stove.

A TIME TO BURN

Don't burn all your bridges.
I can still hear my daddy's words
echoing in my head.
Such a funny expression really,
but I always knew what he meant.
There's a certain diplomacy
in the way you walk away
from a sleazy boss,
a crazy ex-(whatever),
the self-indulgent twit.
There could be advantages
in keeping some bridges intact,
I suppose—
but you'll know, without a doubt,
when it's time to toss a match
and watch the planks
            go down in flames.

TODAY I WILL EAT POTATO CHIPS

and not count calories
or review salt ratios
or work myself into a frenzy
about how many sit ups
it will take to undo the damage;

I will lounge on my deck
in a chair that reclines,
with the sun on my face,
absorbing vitamin D
that doesn't come from a bottle.

Music will float from speakers
and join the birds' concerto
in the windblown leaves;
hummingbirds will chitter
as they sip from sugary feeders.

Today I will live,
lick salt from my fingers,
and throw away
the empty bag.

WHERE I BELONG

In my dream
I searched for the key
to heaven's golden gate
when I stumbled upon
the feet of the one
who died on the cross
for all.
I cried aloud,
a wailing sound,
that rode on angel's wings.
"I don't belong"
said I to He,
"I've done wrong;"
He took my hands,
His, warm as sand,
told me to rise,
to meet His eyes;
I found such kindness there.
"No one does," said He to me;
but don't you see,
that's why I hung
between two thieves,
why I lay in a tomb
until day three,
why I rolled the stone away.
I rose victoriously
so you could come to me.

My lamb, my child
it was for you I died,
and it's you I welcome home.

WHO SAYS

Who says you can't get there from here?
Who says you're destined to be this or that?
There's a box with your name on it,
waiting for you step inside,
      stay inside,
a black and white picture;
color inside the lines,
      inside the lines.
But what if you don't listen?
What if you chop your way
through a rainforest?
What if you rearrange the square
into a triangle,
or launch stars into the midnight sky,
using glitter and a slingshot?
What if you scribble with all your might
and create a masterpiece
that would turn Picasso's head?

WITHOUT SAYING A WORD

Curled into myself,
a snail without a shell,
mascara on my pillowcase.
I want to pray,
but the words won't come.
What do I say
to the Almighty,
He who formed the world
with words?
My words form nothing;
incoherent babblings
about the things I wish
to change:
light to banish darkness,
the removal of stones
from weary shoulders,
fear that sits in my stomach
like wet towels.
I lie there, silently pleading
until I feel His blanket of grace:
I've got you.
I've got this.
Wipe your eyes.
You are the daughter
of a King.

ACKNOWLEDGEMENTS

(The) Big Window Review
"Candles" (March 14, 2023, on-line)

Borrowed Solace
"And The World Moves On" (Issue 5.2 Fall 2023)

Blue Collar Review
"I Carry the Weight" (Spring 2023)

Calliope
"Make Space" (Winter 2023 Issue)

Contemporary Haibun Online
"Left Field" (Issue 19 April 2023)

Drifting Sands Haibun
"Flash in the Pan" (Issue 20 March 2023)
"A Little Lazarus" (Issue 24 November 2023)
"The Other Side" (Issue 21 May 2023)
"Pilgrimage" (Issue 23 Sept. 2023)

Failbetter.com
"Family Reunion" (online October 26, 2023)

Founder's Favourites
"Between" (Issue 22 March 2023)
"When Foxes Play" (Issue 22 March 2023)

ACKNOWLEDGEMENTS

Fresh Words: An International Literary Magazine
"Carry the Wish Seed" (Vol 3, Number 2 Feb. 2023)
"Patched" (Vol 3, Number 2 Feb. 2023)
"A Time to Burn" (Vol 3, Number 2 Feb. 2023)

Garfield Lake Review
"Stopping in the Woods with Frost" (2023 Edition)

Gyroscope Review
"No New Normal" (Summer Issue 2023)

Halcyon Days
"The Art of Being" (Issue 31 October 2023)
"Summer Triolet" (Issue 29 March 2023)
"Writing Muses" (Issue 29 March 2023)

Havik
"Water Fresh and Salt" (May 2023)
"Brain Storm" (May 2023)

Heart
"Left Hanging" (Issue 18)—Winner Honorable Mention

Kurt Vonnegut Museum and Library So it Goes (October 2023)
"Lessons from Mrs. P"

Last Leaves Magazine
"The Fatted Calf" (Issue 7 October 2023)
"Gaunt" (Issue 6 April 2023)
"Grandma's Sunday Kitchen" (Issue 7 October 2023)

ACKNOWLEDGEMENTS

Literary Heist
"Battles Unseen" (online Sept. 21, 2023)
"The Cycle" (online June 21, 2023)

Mockingheart Review
"The Self-Made Poet" (online June 1, 2023)

Modern Literature
"Aging: Not for the Faint of Heart" (online 8/9/2023)
"Grief" (online 8/9/2023)
"Hats Off to" (online 2/9/2023)
"Hitchhiking to the Stars" (online 2/9/2023)
"I Heard a Fly Buzz" (online 8/9/2023)
"Lake Erie in Ashtabula" (online 8/9/2023)
"Location" (online 2/9/2023)
"Nothing at All" (online 2/9/2023)
"Origami" (online 8/9/2023)
"Porch Summers" (online 8/9/2023)
"Redial" (online 8/9/2023)
"Sweeping" (online 2/9/2023)
"What the World Sees" (online 2/9/2023)

Mudlark
"Civilization" (Fall 2023)
"Genetics" (Fall 2023)
"State of the Human Address" (Fall 2023)

North of Oxford
"A Different Kind of Hunger" (June 7, 2023)
"Truth be Told" (June 7, 2023)

ACKNOWLEDGEMENTS

October Hill Magazine
"Fanning the Flames" (Vol 7, Issue 1 Spring 2023)
"Getting Orders" (Vol 7, Issue 3 Fall 2023)
"We Came Back" (Vol 7, Issue 1 Spring 2023)

Orchard's Poetry Journal
"Lake Triolet" (Summer Issue 2023)

Rat's Ass Review
"The Decline of Old Detroit" (Fall-Winter 2023 Issue)

Remington Review
"In This God-Forsaken Place" (Fall 2023 Issue)

Right Hand Pointing (Ambidextrous Press)
"That Moment" (Oct. 2023 Issue)

Shark Reef
"The Edge of Remembering" (Fall 2023 Issue)

Shot Glass Journal
"Breakthrough" (Issue 40 2023)

Southern Florida Poetry Journal (SoFloPoJo)
"Silencer" (Feb. 2, 2023)

Smokey Blue Literary and Arts Magazine
"Church Campground Reunion" (Issue 18 March 1, 2023)

Time of Singing
"Under the Canopy" (Vol 50, Number 2 Summer 2023)

ACKNOWLEDGEMENTS

Tipton Poetry Review
"Before Social Media" (Jan. 2023)

Triggerfish Critical Review
"I Am Nobody" (forthcoming in Issue 31 Jan. 2024)

ABOUT THE AUTHOR

Arvilla Fee has been married for over twenty-one years to Colonel James Fee and has six biological, officially (and unofficially) adopted children: Kara, Kyle, Armoni, Jennica, Alec, and D'Andre, her daughter-in-law, Stephanie, her sweet granddaughter, Embree, and another grandchild, Ryland on the way—all of whom she counts as her greatest blessings. She has had a long academic career, receiving a Bachelor's degree in the Science of Education from IUPUI, a Master's of Education from Weber State, and a Master's of Liberal Arts English from Auburn University at Montgomery. She has taught English in middle schools, high schools, and colleges, including her current position as an English adjunct at Clark State College. She has been published in numerous presses including *Contemporary Haibun Online, Drifting Sands Haibun, Remington Review, Shot Glass Journal, North of Oxford, Mudlark, Havik, Gyroscope, Rat's Ass Review, Modern Literature, Right Hand Pointing, Halcyon Days, Tipton Poetry Review, Last Leaves Magazine, Garfield Lake Review, October Hill Magazine* and many others.

Arvilla writes about life in its raw, unvarnished, messy state, based on her own trauma as well as the trauma she had witnessed in others. Having experienced abuse, divorce, toxic relationships, the death of loved ones, the death of her beloved dog, a miscarriage, family members struggling with addiction, the sorrow and pain of her students, exhaustion from raising children and growing older, and witnessing different cultures around the globe, she has a true, empathetic connection to others. For Arvilla, poetry has never been about gaining elite literary status but about being in the trenches with ordinary people who will say, *"She gets me."*

Printed in the USA
CPSIA information can be obtained
at www.ICGtesting.com
LVHW011638250324
775427LV00007B/120